Kingfisher Books, Grisewood & Dempsey Ltd
Elsley House, 24-30 Great Titchfield Street,
London W1P 7AD

First published in 1993 by Kingfisher Books
10 9 8 7 6 5 4 3 2 1

BRITISH LIBRARY CATALOGUING IN PUBLICATION DATA
A catalogue record for this book is available from the
British Library.

ISBN 0 86272 944 0

Editors: Nicola Barber and Andrea Moran
Senior Designer: Ralph Pitchford
Designers: Michèle Arron, Sandra Begnor, Paul
Richards
Cover artwork by Kuo Kang Chen

Phototypeset by Southern Positives and Negatives
(SPAN), Lingfield, Surrey
Printed in Italy

The publishers wish to thank the following artists for
contributing to this book:

Jonathan Adams: pp. 33 (bottom), 36 (right), 52 (centre
right), 101 (top), 108/109, 116 (left), 131 (left), 137 (top
right), 139 (bottom left); Owain Bell: p. 34 (right); Dennis
Bosdet: pp. 60 (bottom), 61 (bottom left), 115 (top left);
Peter Bull: p. 68; Tony Chance (Garden Studios): p. 76;
Kuo Kang Chen: pp. 15, 19 (top), 22 (bottom), 23
(bottom), 25 (top left), 26 (right), 27 (top), 30, 34
(bottom), 44 (top), 51 (bottom right), 61 (centre left), 62,
63 (bottom), 75, 76 (left), 77 (left), 78 (centre left), 84, 87,
89 (left), 103 (centre), 104, 105, 118/119, 121, 123
(bottom right), 126 (top right), 130 (top), 134 (right), 135
(top), 137 (bottom), 138, 140 (top left), 150 (centre), 153;
Peter Dennis (Linden Artists): pp. 7, 26 (centre and top),
28 (bottom), 46/47, 66, 80 (bottom left), 105 (bottom),
125, 131 (centre), 148/149; Mark Franklin: pp. 29 (top
left), 38 (bottom), 59 (right), 98 (top), 99 (left); Jeremy
Gower: pp. 6 (left), 12 (top), 17 (right), 24 (left), 25
(bottom), 35 (top right), 49, 57 (top right), 58, 63 (top),
73, 80, 85 (left), 88 (left), 92, 94, 96 (top), 106, 107
(bottom), 110 (centre right), 111 (top), 120 (right), 126
(left), 133, 150 (bottom right), 152; Ian Howatson: p. 65
(left), 77 (right), 100 (top), 102 (top), 107 (left), 142 (top);
Valerie Sangster (Linden Artists): pp. 60/61, 115 (top left);
Mike Saunders: (Kathy Jakeman Illustration) pp. 10/11,
18 (top), 19 (bottom), 56 (bottom); John Scorey: pp. 28,
95, 136, 145

The publishers would also like to thank Joan Angelbeck,
Peter Barber, Ian Graham, Tracey McNerney and Frazer
Swift for their invaluable assistance.

KINGFISHER
FIRST
ENCYCLOPEDIA OF
SCIENCE

BRIAN J. FORD

Kingfisher Books

abacus

The abacus is the world's oldest type of COMPUTER. It is made of beads on wires. The first row of beads stands for ones, then tens, next hundreds, and so on. By moving beads to the central bar and adding the beads in each row you can do arithmetic. The first abacus was used in Babylon 5000 years ago. But Japanese workers still use them in electronics factories. An abacus can sometimes give an answer quicker than a CALCULATOR.

▼ Numbers are multiplied or divided on an abacus by moving beads across to the vertical dividing bar. Adding their values gives the total.

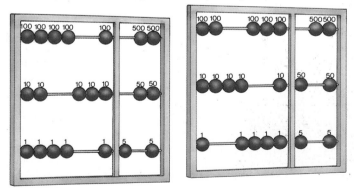

abrasive

Fine, hard substances that wear down solids such as wood, metal or stone, are called abrasives. Sandpaper is covered with an abrasive.

absolute zero

Absolute zero is –273.16°C or 0 K (Kelvin). This is the TEMPERATURE when there is no HEAT ENERGY present.

absorption

Many substances can soak up a liquid. A towel does this when you dry yourself. This is absorption. HEAT, LIGHT and SOUND can also be absorbed. Light colours are cooler to wear on a hot day, as they absorb less heat than dark colours.

acceleration

Acceleration means 'getting faster'. If you stop (on your bike, for instance) and then start riding again, you accelerate. When you put on the brakes to slow down the opposite happens, you decelerate.

▼ Boiling a red cabbage in water makes an acid/alkali indicator. Alkalis (baking powder) turn the indicator green. Acids (vinegar) turn it pink.

acid and alkali

Acids are active chemicals which always contain at least one ATOM of HYDROGEN. But they can pass on this hydrogen very easily. Alkalis are active chemicals which accept hydrogen atoms, in exchange for the metal atoms they contain. So acids and alkalis react together, to form SALTS. Vinegar and lemon juice are weak acids. Baking powder is a weak alkali, but oven cleaners contain very strong alkalis. Strong acids and alkalis burn the skin.

ACID RAIN

Rain has always been acid. It reacts with the carbon dioxide and sulphur dioxide released by bacteria to form a weak acid. It measures about six on the pH scale. But the acidic fumes from burning coal and oil make rain much more acidic. Acid rain measures pH 3 to 5.5 and can damage plant life. Lakes in some countries have lost most of their animal life because of acid rain.

DID YOU KNOW?

The natural acids in rain mean that rainwater dissolves limestone rock. This is how caves are formed. The effect of acid rain means that the stone used to make buildings can be attacked. Some famous buildings have been damaged by acid rain. And many statues are now unrecognizable.

▶ It is our demand for goods and energy which creates acid rain. Power stations, factories and cars that burn fossil fuels produce huge amounts of acidic gases each day.

The gases from an industrial area can travel thousands of miles before they produce acid rain. Many places suffering from acid rain are far from the countries which cause it.

gases react with rainwater and produce acid rain

gases carried by wind

waste gases produced by factories, power plants and car exhausts

acid rain damages forests and pollutes streams and lakes

▶ Acid rain has damaged forests in North America, Europe and Scandinavia.

7

A

adhesives

Adhesives stick objects together. We still do not understand what makes things 'sticky'. Modern adhesives include resins and superglue. The oldest adhesives were made from plants, or by boiling bones and animal hooves.

adsorption

Some substances can adsorb on to a solid. This means they stick on the outside. If you can smell smoke on your jumper, it is because the smoke particles have been adsorbed onto the fibres.

aerosol

An aerosol is a fine mist of particles suspended in a gas. When you sneeze, you make an aerosol of saliva and germs. A scent spray makes an aerosol of perfume. The word aerosol is also used to describe a can, filled with a liquid (or powder) product such as paint or deodorant, and a pressurized gas called a propellant. When the button is pressed, the pressure inside forces the liquid to spray out in a fine mist. See **chlorofluorocarbons**.

▼ Pressing the button on an aerosol can releases the pressure inside. The propellant forces the liquid to spray out in a fine mist.

aerosol spray   button   nozzle

valve closed

valve open

liquid and propellant under pressure

air see **pages 10 and 11**

air conditioning

A REFRIGERATOR system and a HEAT EXCHANGER are used to keep the air in a building the same temperature winter and summer. Air conditioning uses a lot of energy.

aircraft

As a plane speeds along the runway, its wings cut the air. When it reaches the take-off speed, the whole plane lifts off the ground and starts to fly. An aircraft can fly because the AIR is thick. Hinged panels on the main wings are called flaps. The flaps produce extra lift. They are put down to help the plane fly slowly, near the ground. On the smaller wings at the rear of the plane are the elevators. These tip the nose of the plane up or down. At the back is the tail-fin. It has a flap, called the rudder, which is used to turn the plane left or right.

The first planes were very light, like the WRIGHT FLYER, the world's first aircraft. These planes had small petrol engines and propellers to draw them through the air. Later the jet engine was invented. This is a TURBINE. A large fan draws in a stream of air. The air is mixed with fuel and burns, producing a massive thrust of

DID YOU KNOW?

A plane built in 1904 by Horatio Phillips had 20 wings. It looked a bit like a bicycle with a huge venetian blind on top of it. Several years later Count Caproni built a huge flying houseboat with 18 wings. It was as big as a block of flats, but was wrecked when it tried to take off. The first aeroplane to take off under its own power (carrying a pilot) was the *Eole*, which was flown by Clement Ader in France on 9 October, 1890.

wing span 25.6m
length 62.1m

lift

air flowing over wings

wing tip

tail assembly

fin

rudder

drag

fuselage

cabin

pointed nose and thin wings reduce drag

thrust

gravity

delta shaped wing

hot gas. As the gas rushes out of the jet engine, it passes through a second fan, turning it even faster. This is connected to the fan at the front, and so the jet creates its power. Modern aircraft can fly above the weather and the SUPERSONIC planes, like Concorde, travel in the STRATOSPHERE on the edge of space. Concorde flies faster than a bullet.

alcohol

There are many alcohols, from ethanol in alcoholic drinks to waxy alcohols found in plants. Alcohols are chemicals that contain CARBON, HYDROGEN and OXYGEN. They are used in many manufacturing processes. Most alcohols are poisonous.

▼ Among the uses of alcohols are the production of plastics, cosmetics, paints and varnishes.

cosmetics

plastics

paints and varnishes

▲ Concorde's engines propel it at more than twice the speed of sound. Its special wings reduce the problems of air resistance caused at such high speeds.

alloy

An alloy is a mixture of METALS. Many metals are more useful if they are blended with other metals. Brass is made by alloying COPPER and ZINC. Bronze is made out of copper and tin. ALUMINIUM alloys are much stronger than aluminium on its own. NICKEL and copper alloys are used to make coins, because pure copper is too soft and would wear away.

aluminium

bronze

gold

pewter

brass

gold

steel

▲ Alloys are chosen for their special properties. Aluminium alloys, used in aircraft, are light and strong. Tungsten steel alloys are used to make extremely hard cutting tools.

9

AIR AND ATMOSPHERE

The Earth is covered by air held down by gravity. This is the atmosphere. We live in the thick air at the bottom. It gets thinner as you go up. The first layer is about 15 kilometres deep. This is where the weather occurs. The top of the thinnest layer reaches about 400 kilometres above the ground.

▶ Imagine the gases in the air all separated out in this balloon. Air is mostly nitrogen, the yellow part. Next is oxygen, coloured red. The blue layer is argon. The carbon dioxide is in the bucket hanging over the side.

▶ Satellites orbit 400 kilometres above the Earth. If they were any lower than this, friction with the air would cause them to burn up.

DID YOU KNOW?

Almost four-fifths of the air we breathe is nitrogen. Oxygen, the gas we need to survive, makes up only one-fifth. Argon makes up one percent. There is only one part of carbon dioxide in 3500 parts of air – too small to see on this piechart.

nitrogen

oxygen

argon

A parachutist knows you can use the thickness of air to float down slowly. Without a parachute, the human body falls at 300 kilometres an hour. But the parachute provides air resistance, so the speed is low enough for a safe landing. Parachutists can steer by pulling the cords.

meteors

thermosphere

mesosphere

stratosphere

troposphere

weather patterns

▶ The force of moving air can destroy whole buildings. Tornadoes are violent whirlwinds, with wind speeds of up to 500 kilometres an hour. Winds like this leave a trail of destruction wherever they pass.

satellite

aurora

Concorde

clouds

◀ The top layer of the atmosphere, 400 km above ground, is the thermosphere. It has just a few molecules of air. This is where the aurora occurs.

◀ At 80 km (the mesosphere) the air is thick enough for grains of matter shooting through space to burn up as shooting stars.

◀ Between 15 km and 60 km is the stratosphere, where Concorde flies. High in the stratosphere is the ozone layer, which protects life on Earth from ultraviolet rays.

◀ The lowest layer is the air with which we are surrounded – the troposphere. It is about 10–20 km deep. Weather occurs in the troposphere.

◀ Compared to the Earth, the atmosphere is not very deep. If the Earth was the size of an apple, the atmosphere would only be as thick as the peel.

record player

amplifier

loudspeaker

▲ The amplifier strengthens the signals produced by a record before they are passed to the speakers.

aluminium

Aluminium is the third commonest ELEMENT in the EARTH'S crust. It is found as an ORE. It is very light and is used to make AIRCRAFT. When first discovered aluminium was used like a precious METAL, to make jewellery.

▼ Aluminium can be hammered into thin sheets of foil or drawn out into wires to make electrical cables. It is also used to make window frames, fizzy drink cans and firefighters' suits.

ammeter

The flow of a current of ELECTRICITY is measured in amperes (amps), using an ammeter. The symbol for amperes is A.

ammonia

Ammonia is a gas. Each molecule contains one ATOM of NITROGEN and three of HYDROGEN. Its formula is NH_3. It dissolves in water to produce ammonia SOLUTION, an ALKALI which gives off choking fumes. Ammonia is used to make fertilizers, and coolants for REFRIGERATORS.

amplifier

The electrical signals produced by MICROPHONES are weak. To produce sound from a LOUDSPEAKER they must be made stronger, or amplified. Using TRANSISTORS or INTEGRATED CIRCUITS, an amplifier magnifies a weak electrical signal. Musicians who play the electric guitar plug into an 'amp' (short for amplifier). Then the small vibrations of the strings can produce a huge sound from the loudspeaker.

analogue

An analogue is a model. The figures around a watch dial are an analogue of the passing of time. The height of the MERCURY in a THERMOMETER is an analogue of your temperature. See **digital**.

antifreeze

Some chemicals lower the TEMPERATURE at which water turns to ICE. These chemicals can be used as an antifreeze. SALT is one example, and in car ENGINES ethanediol (ethylene glycol) is used. This is an ALCOHOL, and is very poisonous.

aqualung

Taking a tank of compressed air under water to supply a diver seems easy. But water PRESSURE increases with depth. If the air the diver breathes is at a different pressure to the surrounding water, the diver's lungs could easily collapse or burst. An aqualung has a constant pressure valve which allows the diver to breathe easily at different depths.

pressure valve

air tanks

flippers

air hose

face mask

◄ The aqualung, invented in 1943 by Emile Gagnan for Jacques-Yves Cousteau, enables divers to swim freely underwater.

knife

weighted belt

pressure gauge

LIFE STORY

Archimedes

Archimedes was a Greek philosopher who lived more than 2000 years ago. The king had told him to find out whether the new crown had been made with pure GOLD, or if some SILVER had been added. Archimedes knew that if the crown contained silver it would be lighter. He thought of comparing the volume of the crown with the volume of a piece of gold of the same weight. But how could he MEASURE the volume of the crown? The answer came to him one day as he stepped into a full bath and saw the water flow over the edge. He realized that the volume of water the crown would displace would equal the volume of the crown. Archimedes was so excited that he ran home without dressing, shouting 'Eureka! Eureka!' (Greek for 'I've found it').

argon

Argon is a gas that is similar to NEON, and never forms COMPOUNDS. It is called an 'inert' or 'noble' gas. Argon is the third commonest gas in the ATMOSPHERE, making up one percent of the air.

arithmetic see **mathematics**

arsenic

Arsenic is an ELEMENT that is a bit like a METAL. It exists in several different forms: metallic arsenic, black or brown arsenic and yellow arsenic. It is a slow poison and has been used in the past for many famous murders.

artificial intelligence see **computer**

asbestos

There are several types of asbestos. It is a soft fibrous MINERAL that will resist HEAT. One use of asbestos is in brake linings for cars, trains and planes. It has also been used for heat insulation. But people who breathe in asbestos dust can develop a disease known as asbestosis. We now know that people can even develop cancer many years after breathing the dust. So asbestos has been removed from many buildings. This leaves a lot of dust in the air, so the job must be done carefully.

asteroid see **Solar System**

astronaut see **spacecraft**

astronomy
Astronomy is the science of studying space. People long ago used to watch the stars, and knew their positions in the night sky. If a new STAR appeared, its position

was noted on a star MAP. The first COMET was drawn in this way, more than 2000 years ago. Astronomers use telescopes to study the planets more closely. Today, SPACECRAFT can also land cameras on the planets to make close-up studies of their surfaces and atmospheres.

atmosphere see **pages 10 and 11**

atom see **page 15**

Ptolemy's universe

Copernicus' universe

▲ Ancient Greek astronomers believed that the Earth was at the centre of the Universe. Their ideas survived until the 16th century when a Polish churchman, Nikolai Kopernik (known to us as Copernicus), proved that the Earth and all the other planets revolve around the Sun.

aurora
The Sun sends out waves of ENERGY. This energy is drawn towards the North and South magnetic POLES of the Earth. Sometimes there is enough energy to produce an aurora. This is a flickering curtain of light in the night sky. Auroras are usually seen near to the Poles, but can sometimes be seen in countries thousands of kilometres away.

14

ATOMS AND MOLECULES

An atom is the smallest piece of an element. A million atoms would measure one millimetre across. The smallest atom is that of hydrogen. Among the largest is uranium, which is over 200 times heavier than hydrogen. Atoms contain a lot of energy. When they are split, this energy can be released. This principle is used to make nuclear weapons and electricity.

▼ The protons have a positive electric charge. The neutrons have no charge at all. Inside each of these particles are three smaller bodies. These are quarks. The forces which stick the quarks together are known as 'gluons'.

▼ The negatively charged electrons orbit at fixed distances from the nucleus. Each layer of electrons makes up an electron shell.

▼ At the centre of the atom is the nucleus, containing protons and neutrons. Electrons orbit the nucleus. They are much smaller than in this picture. With a nucleus this size, the electrons would be the size of pin-heads orbiting over a kilometre away!

electron

neutron

proton

orbit of electron

MOLECULES AND CRYSTALS

A molecule is the smallest piece of a compound that can exist. The molecule below shows a molecule of water.

oxygen

hydrogen

Atoms of sodium and chlorine link to form cubic crystals of salt.

sodium — chlorine

This twisted molecule is the most important to every form of life – DNA.

15

B

balloon

Two types of balloons can rise in the AIR. One is filled with a gas which is lighter than air, such as HYDROGEN or HELIUM. Hydrogen is lighter than helium, but it catches fire easily. Helium does not burn and is therefore safer to use. The other type is filled with hot air. The balloon rises because hot air is lighter than cold air. The balloons you blow up at parties make a loud bang when they burst.

bar code see page 17

barium

Barium is a metal whose ATOMS block X-RAYS. Doctors give a patient a barium 'meal' to swallow when they want to look for any odd shapes in the soft intestines.

barometer

From hour to hour the PRESSURE of the AIR around us changes. If it's going up, finer weather is due. If it falls, expect rain. A barometer measures air pressure, and shows the results on a dial. The first barometers had a column of mercury supported by air pressure. Aneroid barometers have a metal chamber which changes shape as the air pressure goes up and down.

battery

A battery contains chemicals that react and produce ELECTRICITY. The first battery was made by Alessandro Volta, an Italian scientist. Alkaline cells (the modern batteries you use in a torch or personal stereo) are very long-lasting. Some special small batteries can be recharged. Cars have a lead-acid battery, which can be recharged. See **volt**.

negative terminal

positive terminal

plates

wet battery

▲ A car battery contains two sets of plates standing in sulphuric acid. One set is made from lead, the other from lead dioxide. Reactions between the acid and the plates produce an electric current.

▼ Torches use a type of battery called a dry cell. The acid is in the form of a paste so that it cannot spill out. In one type of dry cell there is a zinc outer case and a carbon rod in the centre.

dry battery

carbon rod

zinc container

chemical paste (acid)

BAR CODE

Bar codes are printed stripes of black and white. They appear on supermarket goods and are used on library books. Bar codes are even used on hospital specimens. They do not hold any mysterious information. They are just a list of code numbers and letters from a catalogue. The advantage of using bar codes is that they can be read automatically, by computer.

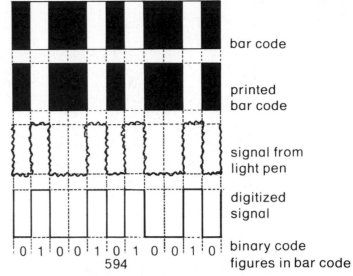

bar code

printed bar code

signal from light pen

digitized signal

0 1 0 0 1 0 1 0 0 1 0   binary code figures in bar code

594

▲ The computer reads the number of bands in a bar code. It measures how wide they are. The computer can then translate the digital signal back into numbers.

▶ Bar codes can be printed upright, or lying down. The upright ones are known as 'ladder' bar codes, as the stripes of the code look like a ladder. The horizontal bar codes are called 'picket fence' codes.

picket fence bar code

upright bar code

▲ The check number confirms that the code was read properly.

▲ Here is the catalogue number.

◀ This is the number of the company which produced the goods.

9 314118 6215 3

7

◀ The code starts with a digit that indicates the country of origin.

▲ Bar codes can be read with a hand-held wand. A laser beam is shone down the wand. The scanner picks up the light reflected from the bars, and produces a digital signal which is passed to a computer. The computer can match the information to an entry in the catalogue.

reflected light

angled laser beam

▲ The wand must be held at an angle, or the reflection is too bright to be read.

▼ In a supermarket the bar code is read as an item passes over a laser beam. To make sure the code is read properly, the laser beam scans back and forth dozens of times in a fraction of a second. The computer can then check that the readings are correct.

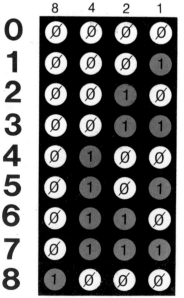

▲ The Big Bang was a vast explosion. Matter and radiation were thrown out in all directions. Then the Universe expanded and cooled, and the galaxies formed.

Big Bang

The Big Bang is the name given to the theory that says the UNIVERSE began with a gigantic explosion 15,000 million years ago, and that the galaxies are still moving apart from the explosion. One piece of evidence for this theory is that distant stars seem to give off red light, as though they are moving away from us. The universe may expand forever, or it may stop and then slowly collapse in on itself.

binary

A binary system has only two positions 'on' (1) and 'off' (0). By using combinations of 1 and 0, you can make any figure. So, 'one' would be 001, and 'two' 010. Then 'three' would be one plus two, or 011. This idea lies at the root of the DIGITAL systems used by COMPUTERS and in RECORDINGS.

	8	4	2	1
0	Ø	Ø	Ø	Ø
1	Ø	Ø	Ø	1
2	Ø	Ø	1	Ø
3	Ø	Ø	1	1
4	Ø	1	Ø	Ø
5	Ø	1	Ø	1
6	Ø	1	1	Ø
7	Ø	1	1	1
8	1	Ø	Ø	Ø

◄ Our counting system is based on the numbers 0 to 9, ten numbers in all. Binary code is a counting system based on the number two. It is better suited to computers because their circuits have two states, off and on. These two states are used to represent the numbers 0 and 1.

binoculars

If you strap two TELESCOPES together you can make a pair of binoculars. Binoculars are easier to use than a telescope because you are using both eyes to look at the same image.

biochemistry

Biochemistry is the study of the chemicals connected with life. Living things contain many COMPOUNDS of the ELEMENTS nitrogen carbon, oxygen and hydrogen. Biochemists study the structure of these compounds, and what they do inside the cells of living things. By studying the reactions of these compounds, biochemists have found cures and treatments for many diseases.

black hole

When a massive STAR ages it begins to contract. As its MASS shrinks into a smaller VOLUME, its field of GRAVITY gets stronger and stronger. This increased gravitational force makes the star collapse into a smaller and smaller volume. Eventually, the gravity is so strong that even light cannot escape. Astronomers can only detect the star by its effect on other bodies in space – they cannot see it because no light escapes. This 'invisible star' is a black hole.

rubber gloves

bleach

▲ Tie a coloured T-shirt with string. Wearing rubber gloves, soak the shirt for 30 minutes in a weak solution of bleach to give a tie-dye effect.

bleach

Many coloured chemicals lose their colour when they react with OXYGEN. COMPOUNDS which cause this effect are called bleaches. At home, one common bleach is hydrogen peroxide, used to lighten hair. Another is chlorine bleach, used in the kitchen. Bleach combines with and destroys any BIOCHEMICAL compound. Since germs are made of biochemical MOLECULES, bleach is a valuable aid to killing germs.

▼ The immense gravity of a black hole may distort light from nearby stars.

black hole

red supergiant

collapsing star

▼ CAT scanners are used to detect problems such as tumours inside a patient's body. X-rays are fired through a section of the body at different angles. The patient feels nothing. The x-rays are received by detectors and combined by a computer to produce the final image.

computer image

computer

tumour

x-rays scan section of brain

electrical power

body scanner

body scanner

A body scanner produces pictures of sections of a living person. There are several types of scanner. The CAT-scanner fires X-RAY beams through the patient to a detector. Information is sent to a computer which then builds up a picture of part of the body. A magnetic resonance scanner uses the PROTON in the hydrogen atoms of each WATER molecule inside the body. A system of MAGNETS makes the protons RESONATE, and a picture can be built up of soft internal organs.

boiling

Boiling is when a bubbling liquid changes to a gas. The boiling point of WATER is 100°C or 373 K.

bubbles

Bubbles are pockets of gas trapped inside a solid or liquid. Some cheese has bubbles from the microbes which made it. Bubbles can be made by dipping a wire loop into SOAP solution. If you shape a wire coat-hanger, you can make bubbles that start out as strange shapes – even square ones!

▼ Soap bubbles are round. The skin is tight, because of surface tension. It is trying to pull inwards against the air inside. The weight of the water in the bubbles can make them oval, and when two are joined the surfaces between them are flat.

liquid detergent

| **burning** see **combustion**

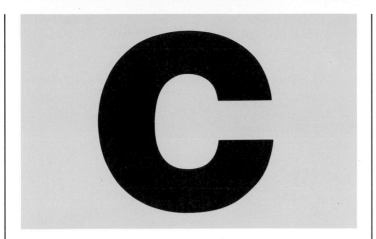

C

caffeine

Caffea is the Latin name for the coffee plant. Caffeine means 'in coffee'. It is a DRUG you find in coffee. Pure caffeine forms white crystals. This drug makes the heart beat faster and can also cause headaches. Caffeine keeps people awake. It is found in other drinks too. For instance, a cup of tea and even a glass of cola contain some caffeine!

calcium

Calcium is a very reactive METAL. It is never found on its own in nature. But COMPOUNDS of calcium are very common in rocks, such as limestone and marble.

▶ Calcium salts are found in many forms. The fur in a kettle is needle-shaped crystals of calcium sulphate. Calcite and seashells contain calcium carbonate.

They are also found in dairy foods, like cheese. Salts of calcium are used to make strong bones and teeth, which is why they are important for your health.

calculator

Calculators contain a MICROCHIP which can do difficult calculations in an instant. As the chip is very small, a tiny calculator can even be fitted inside a watch. Some calculators are powered by SOLAR ENERGY.

light-emitting display

electric circuit

▲ Electronic calculators contain a tiny microchip that can add, subtract, multiply and divide large numbers in an instant. Scientific calculators can be programmed to do more difficult calculations. Numbers are displayed on light-emitting diodes or a liquid crystal display.

▼ Limestone is a soft rock made from the calcium-rich shells of millions of microscopic sea creatures. Rainwater dissolves the soft rocks, forming channels which eventually join up and form a complicated network of underground tunnels and waterways.

1

2

3

calendar

This is how we mark the passing of days. The time it takes the EARTH to go around the Sun is a YEAR. The MOON goes from New Moon to New Moon in 29.53 days. And the Earth turns right around once a DAY. The earliest calendars used the Moon's month to work out the length of a year. But 12 lunar (Moon) months make only 354 days. To make the total up to 365, most months have 30 or 31 days.

camera

Cameras capture an image of the outside world, and produce a picture. A VIDEO camera or camcorder records moving pictures by electronics. A camera used for PHOTOGRAPHY takes pictures on FILM.

carbon

Soot is carbon, and so is coal. Carbon is a non-metallic ELEMENT. It forms thousands of different COMPOUNDS. Most of the compounds in your body contain carbon.

▶ Carbon atoms in sheets form soft graphite (in the pencil). Joined in a strong lattice they make diamond. It has even been shown that carbon atoms can join in spheres, which have been nick-named 'buckyballs'.

carbon dating

Natural carbon contains an ISOTOPE, produced by COSMIC RAYS. This decays with a HALF-LIFE of 5760 years. Measuring how much carbon-14 is left helps to find out the age of ancient remains.

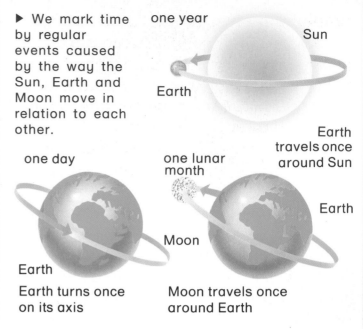

▶ We mark time by regular events caused by the way the Sun, Earth and Moon move in relation to each other.

one year

Sun

Earth

Earth travels once around Sun

one day

one lunar month

Earth

Earth turns once on its axis

Moon

Earth

Moon travels once around Earth

carbon dioxide

Carbon dioxide is a rare gas in the AIR. There is only one part of carbon dioxide in 3000 parts of air! Its formula is CO_2 (one carbon and two oxygen atoms). See **greenhouse effect**.

cassette see **recording, video**

catalyst

Catalysts are strange substances that help CHEMICAL reactions to take place. But the catalyst itself is not changed or used up in the reaction.

▼ A sugar cube makes lemonade fizz violently. It acts like a catalyst, helping bubbles to form.

catalytic converter

Fumes from a car exhaust contain poisonous gases. A catalytic converter in the exhaust helps to turn the poisons into safer gases like water vapour and CARBON DIOXIDE. But although a catalytic converter reduces one sort of pollution, it is no answer to the GREENHOUSE EFFECT.

cathode rays

Cathode rays are beams of ELECTRONS. They can only travel in a vacuum. Cathode rays produce the image in an ELECTRON MICROSCOPE. They also make the picture on a TV screen.

▲ A television picture is formed by cathode rays tracing a series of lines on a screen coated with material that glows when hit by electrons.

cellular phone

Ordinary telephones send messages along wires. But cellular phones use radio. They contain a RADIO transmitter, which sends its message to a local relay station. A cellular phone switches automatically to the nearest local station as you travel across the country.

Celsius

Anders Celsius was a Swedish scientist who thought of dividing the TEMPERATURE scale into 100 parts. This lead to the scale we use today, with 100 degrees between the boiling and freezing points of water.

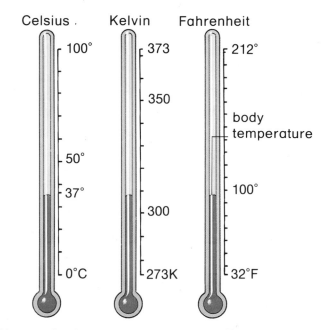

▲ Human body temperature is 37°C on the Celsius scale, 310 K on the Kelvin scale, and 98°F in Fahrenheit.

▼ Each cell has its own relay station which receives calls from a cellular phone.

▲ Cement is made by crushing clay and limestone together, heating the mixture and then grinding it down to make a fine powder.

cement

Cement means 'hard glue'. There is cement in your teeth. Building cement is made by heating limestone and clay. This drives off the WATER (H_2O) and CARBON DIOXIDE (CO_2). In order to use the powdery cement it is mixed with water. It then changes back to its hard, stony form. As it does, the HEAT ENERGY originally put in by the cement furnace is given out. This is why setting cement gets warm.

centrifuge

A centrifuge whirls objects around in a circle at a very high speed. It produces centrifugal force, which pushes the objects

away from the centre as they are spun around. This is what forces water out of wet clothes in a spin drier. Centrifuges can also be used to separate mixtures. If you spin test tubes containing cells they will settle out very quickly. The heavier cells are pushed further outwards and settle at the bottom of the tube. Giant centrifuges are used to train astronauts, as they produce similar forces to a rocket at blast off.

ceramics

Many types of clay are made of tiny grains which melt at high temperatures, just as GLASS does. Ceramic objects are made by firing the moulded clays in a kiln at high temperatures. Examples include porcelain and china. Some special ceramics are used in electronics.

chalk

Millions of minute shelled animals made the chalk cliffs you see today. As they died, their tiny white skeletons or shells built up a thick layer. This hardened to make chalk.

▼ Microscopic shells formed layers at the bottom of the sea and eventually became chalk.

◀ Centrifuges are used to separate liquids and particles in a laboratory and to produce the forces that act on pilots and astronauts in flight.

astronaut training in centrifuge

test tube — motor

speed controls

changes of state

Many substances can exist in different forms. The three states are solids, liquids and gases. If you HEAT a solid it may melt and becomes a liquid. If you heat a liquid it may boil to become a gas. Each step up

gas

liquid

solid

▲ Changes of state are caused by the movement of molecules. When ice is heated the molecules move around and the ice melts to water. On further heating they fly apart, forming a vapour.

uses a lot of HEAT ENERGY. Wax can be seen in all three states when a candle burns. The three states of water are ICE, water and steam. See **combustion.**

charcoal

If you heat wood to a high temperature without letting in OXYGEN, you get charcoal. Charcoal is made of CARBON.

▼ Charcoal is used to purify liquids and gases. As water flows through a filter, impurities are adsorbed on the charcoal, leaving clean water.

water

charcoal   purified water

chemistry see **page 26**

chlorine

Chlorine gas is a greenish-yellow colour and is highly poisonous. It has been used to kill soldiers in war. Some kinds of BLEACH give off chlorine, so they can kill the germs in water, or around a toilet. Chlorine is also used to kill germs in the water supply. When IONS of chlorine join with sodium they form sodium chloride, or common SALT. The sodium and chlorine ions stick together very strongly.

chlorofluorocarbons (CFCs)

Chlorofluorocarbons (CFCs) are gases which contain atoms of chlorine, fluorine and carbon. If they are put in a can under pressure, they change to liquid form. They were used in REFRIGERATORS and as propellants in AEROSOLS. But many people think CFCs damage the OZONE LAYER in the EARTH'S ATMOSPHERE. For this reason, many CFCs are now banned.

▶ When CFCs float up into the stratosphere, their chlorine atoms react with the ozone molecules.

C = carbon
Cl = chlorine
F = fluorine

chlorofluoromethane molecule

chromium

Chromium is one of the hardest and shiniest metals in the world. It resists corrosion and is used in ELECTROPLATING to coat other metals, and also in ALLOYS.

CHEMISTRY

Chemistry is the study of the elements and the compounds they form. Chemists study their properties and also how they react with different substances. Chemicals are everywhere. A substance does not have to be synthetic to be chemical. The food in the kitchen is chemical. Medicines are chemicals too, and many of those were developed from extracts from wild plants. One of the most amazing chemical systems we know about is your body.

▼ Products like flour, baking powder and salt are made with pure ingredients these days as chemists have developed processes to remove impurities. Ground chalk and even lead oxide used to be found in food.

▼ Baking powder and salt are traditional chemicals in your kitchen. But there are many new products, like margarine and the 'creamers' for coffee. Chemical flavourings and preservatives are often added to prepacked foods.

▶ What are the chemical elements in your body? Most of it is oxygen (65 percent – coloured red part in this picture). Carbon, the black part, makes up 18 percent. Next is hydrogen (white) at nine percent, followed by nitrogen (dark blue), at three percent. Two percent of the body is made up of calcium (pale blue) and one percent is phosphorus – the violet toes. Two percent is made up of small amounts of other chemicals. Chemical reactions constantly take place inside your body. Food is 'burnt' with oxygen to give you energy. The vitamins and minerals in your diet are necessary for all the chemical systems to work properly.

iron, iodine, fluorine, zinc and other elements

potassium (0.35%)

sulphur (0.25%)

sodium (0.15%) and magnesium (0.05%)

chlorine (0.2%)

COMPOUNDS

Methane is a compound of carbon and hydrogen. Aluminium chloride has one atom of aluminium to three of chlorine.

methane

aluminium chloride

- carbon
- hydrogen
- chlorine
- aluminium

▲ A cinema film is a plastic strip containing many thousands of separate pictures. The wriggling line down one side of the strip is the film's sound.

cinema

The cinema works because of a trick. If you see a bright image, it takes up to a tenth of a second for the image to fade. You can test this by watching a torch whirling in a circle. Instead of a moving dot, you see a ring of light. This 'persistence of vision' explains how movie films work. Each picture, or frame, moves the action on slightly from the previous one. In the cinema, films are shown at 24 frames a second, so it seems like one continuous movement. On television the films are shown at 25 frames a second – four percent too fast!

circuit

A circuit is a continuous line – like a racing circuit. A current of ELECTRICITY can flow round a circuit in a machine. An electrical circuit can be very simple. All you need to make one is a wire connected to the positive end of a BATTERY, a torch lamp and another wire leading back to the negative end of the battery. The current stops if the circuit is broken. Computers can have thousands of tiny circuits in a single microchip.

▶ The bulb will only light when the switch is closed, completing the circuit.

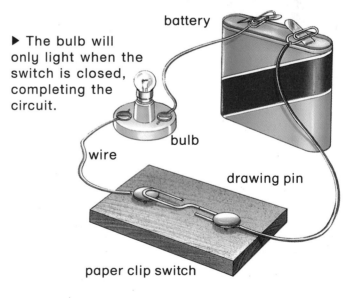

battery

bulb

wire

drawing pin

paper clip switch

circuit breaker

If there is a fault in a circuit which causes an increase in the current, a circuit breaker will cut off the electricity supply to prevent fires or damage to the equipment. See **fuse**.

CLIMATE

Climate is the long-term behaviour of the weather. It results from the bombardment of the atmosphere by endless heat from the Sun. This causes the land and sea to heat and cool, and the resulting movement of air and water create the climate. Temperature and rainfall are the most important factors that determine the climate of a particular area.

WORLD CLIMATES

The world can be divided into climate zones, which depend largely on the distance from the Equator. The **polar climates** are the coldest – at the North and South Poles the average temperature never rises above freezing. In high altitudes there are the clear skies and heavy snow typical of **mountain climates**.

The most important climates to humans are the **temperate** and **tropical climate** zones. These areas are where most people live. The temperate climate is typical of areas away from the equator, where the summers are warm and the winters are mild. The tropics are marked by high humidity and high temperatures.

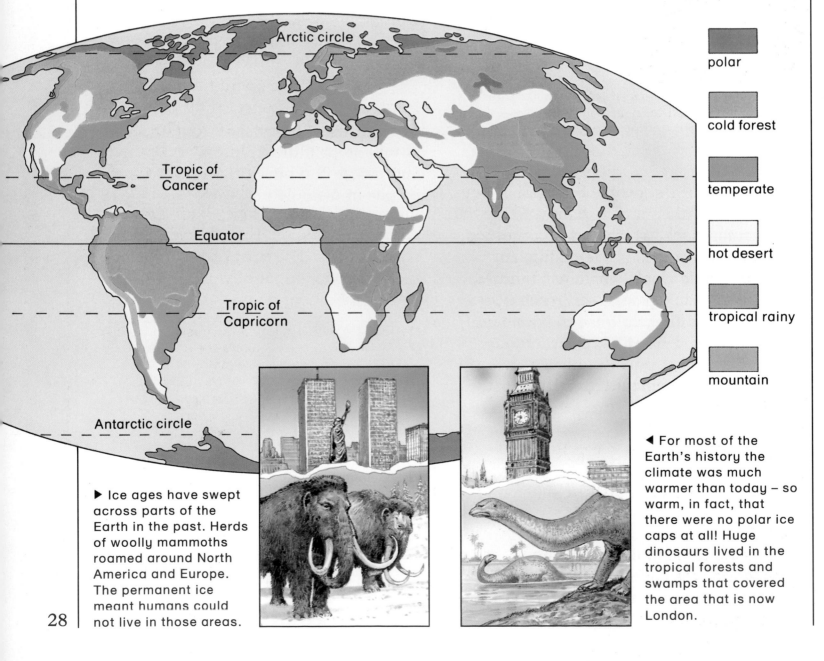

polar

cold forest

temperate

hot desert

tropical rainy

mountain

▶ Ice ages have swept across parts of the Earth in the past. Herds of woolly mammoths roamed around North America and Europe. The permanent ice meant humans could not live in those areas.

◀ For most of the Earth's history the climate was much warmer than today – so warm, in fact, that there were no polar ice caps at all! Huge dinosaurs lived in the tropical forests and swamps that covered the area that is now London.

sundial

water clock

hour glass

pendulum clock

quartz watch

atomic clock

▲ These are just a few of the methods that people have used to measure the passing of time and divide the day into smaller units of time.

clock

In ancient times, people had many ways of marking the passing of time. One was the water clock, which was a container with water dripping out steadily. Another was a candle clock, which used marks down the side of a candle. When gear-wheels were invented, it was possible to design a wind-up clock. Many modern clocks use a CRYSTAL of QUARTZ which will RESONATE at a constant speed. Quartz clocks are very accurate.

cloth and weaving see page 30

cloud see water, weather

coal

Three hundred million years ago much of the world was covered with tropical swamps. There was too little OXYGEN in the swamps for the trees to rot away

completely when they died, so the CARBON they contained was left behind. This formed coal. Coal is a FOSSIL FUEL.

▶ The coal deposits that are mined today were once lush forests. When they died they were buried under mud and then rock. Over millions of years, the rotting plant material changed into coal.

coal forest

submerged forest

coal

colour see page 32

combustion

Combustion is the scientific word for burning. If a substance reacts with OXYGEN it may give out HEAT ENERGY. This can be enough to set fire to the rest of the substance. Watch a candle burning. As the FLAME heats the solid wax it melts into liquid oil. Then the heat of the flame changes the oil to VAPOUR, which burns with oxygen. The heat energy given out melts the next layer of wax, and so combustion goes on.

▼ A candle keeps burning because the heat of the flame continuously melts the candle wax and feeds the flame with more fuel.

unburnt carbon

flame

wick

liquid wax

solid wax

CLOTH AND WEAVING

Cloth is also known as fabric. It is made by weaving, felting and knitting. Weaving is a process of crossing threads so that they produce a flat, flexible fabric. Knitting is a way of making cloth with a single string, rather than with two sets of threads. Felting involves pressing fibres together into a sheet, producing non-woven fabrics.

▼ You can see the difference between woven and knitted cloth below. At the top is an example of weaving, with the weft threads crossing over and under the warp. Below is an example of a knitted fabric with linked threads. Fine nylon fibres are knitted together to make tights. Damaged woven cloth tends to form holes. Knitted fabrics run, or ladder, instead.

▼ You can make a hand loom on a wooden frame, or even with an empty shoe-box cut to shape. Wool or acrylic threads are the easiest to use. The threads that run lengthways are the warp, and the cross threads are the weft. You can use a bobbin as the shuttle. A piece of card with alternate slots and holes lifts the warp threads so the shuttle can pass to and fro.

woven fabric

hand loom

warp threads

shuttle

weft threads

frame

woven fabric

knitted fabric

DID YOU KNOW?

Weaving began in Turkey more than 8000 years ago. There were only slight improvements in weaving looms until Joseph Marie Jacquard invented an automatic loom in 1801. It produced complicated woven patterns that were controlled by a set of punched cards. This gave rise to the data system used on early computers.

▲ If a comet's orbit brings it close to the Sun, a cloud of dust and gas is released, which is blown away from the Sun and forms the comet's tail.

comet

For thousands of years people have seen comets in the sky. They are ORBITING lumps of rock and ice which travel round the SOLAR SYSTEM. Comets have a tail of GAS and dust PARTICLES which may be millions of kilometres long. In 1682, Sir Edmund Halley saw a comet, and worked out that it was the same one that was seen in 1531 and 1607. Halley said that the comet would come back regularly, and it did (the most recent sighting was in 1986).

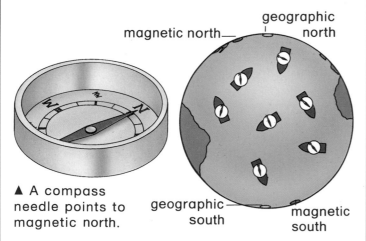

▲ A compass needle points to magnetic north.

compass

The EARTH is like a giant MAGNET with a magnetic field. A magnetic needle will point to the Earth's North POLE. Ancient travellers used natural magnets called lodestones as compasses. Modern navigators know that magnetic north is not exactly at the Earth's geographic North Pole and can adjust their course.

compound

ELEMENTS often join to make compounds. CARBON reacts with OXYGEN to form CARBON DIOXIDE. WATER is a compound of HYDROGEN and oxygen. Oxygen ATOMS form two bonds when they join with other atoms. Carbon forms four; hydrogen only one. That is why there are two oxygens for each carbon atom in carbon dioxide, but one oxygen bonds with two hydrogens in water.

▲ These are molecules of various compounds. All the molecules in a compound are identical, with atoms held together by forces called bonds.

computer see page 34

concrete

Concrete is a mixture of CEMENT and stone. It is harder than cement on its own.

conductor

Heat travels from hot places to cooler ones. It moves quickly through a good conductor. An electrical conductor allows a current to pass through it. Metals are good conductors of HEAT and ELECTRICITY.

COLOUR

The effect of colour is caused by light. Light is made up of different wavelengths. We see each wavelength as a different colour. The longer wavelengths are what we call red, the shortest ones are blue and violet. Solid objects reflect different amounts of each type of light and so they appear to be different colours.

mixing light

primary colours of light

mixing paint

▼ Some people fail to see all colours properly. Their condition is known as colour-blindness. A test using tiny coloured circles can detect colour-blindness.

rainbow

mirror

bevelled edge

primary colours of paint

▲ The bevelled glass at the edge of a mirror can split light into its separate colours. This rainbow effect is the spectrum. The seven main colours of the spectrum are red, orange, yellow, green, blue, indigo and violet.

▲ The primary colours of light are red, green and blue. Together they produce white light. The primary colours of paint or printing ink are red, yellow and blue. Mixed together in exactly equal amounts they make black.

▲ Brightness affects the way we see colours. If you look at the cross above in bright light, it appears bright red on a dark background. In a dim bedroom at dusk, the cross looks black against the palest blue.

DID YOU KNOW?

People always thought that cats and dogs were colour-blind. But recent research shows they can see blue and yellow. Some insects, on the other hand, can see ultraviolet, which is invisible to us. This shows how the same flower appears to a dog, a bee and a person.

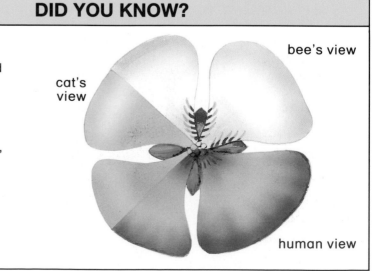

bee's view

cat's view

human view

C

conservation

Conserving means saving. In the past people have captured animals and harvested plants until there were none left. The passenger pigeon of the USA was once common. A flock seen in 1810 contained more than 2000 million birds. But by the year 1900, nearly all the pigeons had been killed. The last one died in 1914. If we are more careful we can prevent this happening to other animals.

Today, many species of plants and animals are in danger of becoming extinct. To conserve them, we need to study their life history. For example, the panda is in danger not because people kill it, but because the bamboo forests in which it lives and feeds are being destroyed. Otters are now rare in Europe because the rivers are polluted. Many species are in danger as the world's rainforests are cleared. These forests are so rich in life that scientists have yet to discover many of the species that live there. These precious habitats need careful management if they and the animals that live there are to survive.

▶ It is important to conserve plants because many of them are useful. This Madagascar periwinkle, for example, has already given us two drugs used to treat cancer. Scientists hope to find other drugs in plants from the rainforests and even in garden weeds.

Madagascar periwinkle

▲ Scorpio and Sagittarius are two of the constellations of the zodiac. This is the path that the Sun is seen to take through the sky each year. It passes through twelve constellations.

constellation

If you look at the night sky you will see that the stars make patterns. In ancient times, people liked to think that these patterns, or constellations, were the marks of gods watching over them, so they gave the star patterns names. In northern skies there is a group of clustered stars called the Seven Sisters, or Pleiades. Another group looks like a saucepan with a bent handle – this is the Great Bear. Three stars in a row are Orion's Belt. The Southern Cross is a constellation of the skies near the South Pole.

continent

The huge masses of land on the Earth's surface are the continents. At the South Pole is the continent of Antarctica. Russia and China cover most of Asia, and America is split into two halves, North and South. India, in the south of Asia, is so large that it is called a sub-continent. About three hundred million years ago the continents were in one big mass. This mass slowly broke up and drifted apart to form the separate continents we know today. See **plate tectonics**.

COMPUTERS

The first small electronic computers were built in Berlin around 1940. A larger machine, called Colossus, was working in Britain in 1943. It had 1500 electron tubes, or valves, to make calculations. Transistors were used in place of valves in the 1950s. Since the development of the microchip in the 1970s, small home computers have become available. The computer at school or in your bedroom has more computing power than all the early models put together.

▼ Business computers used to hold data on large spools of tape. All computers have a central processing unit (CPU) to handle data and a memory to store the information. The data is stored on chips.

▼ A desk-top computer is a vast improvement on the computers of the 1960s. If cars had developed as fast, they could carry hundreds of people at the speed of Concorde using only a spoonful of fuel!

DID YOU KNOW?

Charles Babbage, a British scientist, was a pioneer of computers. He built a 'difference engine' in 1822 to do long calculations, and then went on to design an 'analytical engine' to work out mathematical problems. Sadly, Babbage could not raise enough money for his project and it was never finished.

▼ The keyboard is used to input data, which is then displayed on the screen. The information can be altered or moved using a light pen or a mouse, and then printed out. Some printers can print out in colour.

visual display unit (VDU)

disk drive

printer

screen

▶ The keyboard is used to input data, which is then displayed on the screen. Hard disks can store millions of words.

keyboard

floppy disks

light pen

mouse

convection

Heat can spread through a room by convection. Newly warmed air expands, and so it weighs less than cold air. As a result, it rises into the room. Cooler air then moves in, and is also warmed.

◀ The electrical element inside a kettle heats the water around it. The water expands as it warms. It becomes less dense than the water above it and floats up through the cooler water. This sinks to the bottom, where it is heated, and so convection currents are formed.

copper

Copper is a reddish, rather soft metal, and good CONDUCTOR of heat and electricity. It can be drawn out into fine wires. Copper has long been used to make water pipes. Copper ALLOYS are used to make coins.

corrosion

Metals do not always stay bright and new. They may be damaged by the AIR or by RAIN. IRON, for example, forms RUST if it is exposed to water and air. This is corrosion. Some metals, such as CHROMIUM, hardly ever corrode.

DID YOU KNOW?

Iron only rusts if air and water are both present. In a climate where the humidity of the air is less than 40 percent, iron will never rust! Aluminium forms a thin layer of oxide as soon as it comes in contact with air. This layer means that aluminium always looks slightly dull – but it will not corrode with this built-in protection.

cosmic rays

We are surrounded by RADIATION all our lives. Some comes from space, and this radiation is called 'cosmic rays'. The atmosphere protects us from most of the cosmic rays.

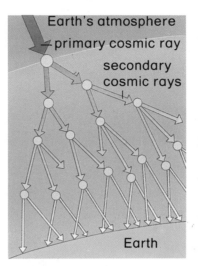

Earth's atmosphere
primary cosmic ray
secondary cosmic rays
Earth

◀ When cosmic rays enter the Earth's atmosphere, they collide with atmospheric particles and secondary cosmic rays are created. This 'avalanche' may continue until the rays reach the ground.

crystals

If MOLECULES or ATOMS stack up in a neat pattern, a crystal may form. You can see ancient crystals of minerals in rocks. At the sea-shore you may find a dried-up rock pool of seawater in which SALT crystals are left behind.

calcite   pyrite   sulphur

▲ Crystals exist in different forms because their atoms or molecules are linked together in different ways. Calcite, pyrite and sulphur show three forms. Snow flakes are also crystals.

C

▲ When an electric light is switched on, electrons which normally orbit atoms in the wire are forced to jump from atom to atom. This forms an electric current.

current

An electric current is a flow of electric charge. It is driven by a POWER source such as a BATTERY. The power source causes ELECTRONS to jump from one ATOM in the wire to the next. The electrons carry an electric charge, and a current flows along the wire. See **electricity, volt**.

cyclone

A cyclone is an area of low air pressure with winds moving around it. It is also known as a 'depression'. An area of high pressure, an anticyclone, has winds moving in the other direction. Cyclonic winds blow anti-clockwise in the Northern Hemisphere but clockwise in the Southern Hemisphere. Near the Equator the winds move in either direction. See **hurricane, isobar, weather**.

36

day and night

The planet EARTH turns on its axis as it orbits the Sun. The Sun constantly shines light at the Earth. The half of the planet which is facing the Sun has day. And the half facing away from the Sun has night.

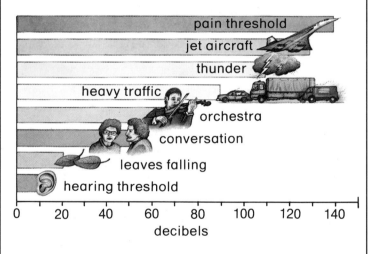

▲ The decibel scale measures sound. Sounds above 140 decibels are painful to hear.

decibel

A decibel is one-tenth of a bel. It is a measure of sound pressure. If a sound reading goes up by ten decibels it means the sound is ten times louder. The bel was named after Alexander Graham Bell. He was born in Scotland in 1847 and went to live in America. He invented the TELEPHONE and an early gramophone.

decimal

Deci- comes from the Latin for 'one-tenth'. The decimal system uses ten as its counting base. Each number stands for units ten times greater than the one to its right. Numbers to the right of the decimal point are fractions. For example, 50 is five tens (fifty), 5.0 is five ones (five), 0.5 is five-tenths (one half).

density

Density is the MASS of a certain volume of a substance. Which do you think weighs most, a kilogram of feathers or a kilogram of lead? Both weigh the same. But the lead has the greater density.

▼ A submarine dives by flooding its 'ballast' tanks to make it denser than the surrounding water. It surfaces by forcing the water out.

submarine surfaces

submarine dives

ballast tank   water in   water out

desalination

Desalination is the process of removing SALT from seawater. To purify seawater it can be BOILED to produce fresh water VAPOUR. When it cools the vapour condenses to form pure water. Another method of desalination uses thin MEMBRANES which hold back the salt from the water. Desalination happens all the time in nature. SOLAR ENERGY evaporates water from the seas, but the salt is left behind. This is why rainwater is fresh. See **distillation**.

desert

Some parts of the EARTH have very little rain. Nothing much grows there. These are the desert areas. Sometimes, when it does rain, masses of beautiful flowers open for just long enough to make seeds.

desertification

Soil contains lots of vegetable matter and tiny living animals and plants. In a desert this living part of the soil is missing. Intensive farming can damage soils, and cause desertification. A warmer, dryer climate also helps deserts to spread.

detergent

Dirt clings to clothing, and water is not enough to remove it. This is because dirt and water often do not mix. Detergents have long MOLECULES. One end of the molecule will stick to grease and dirt, and the other end holds onto the WATER. The molecules of detergent surround the dirt and draw it away. A range of detergents are used. Some are made for washing clothes, others for dishes.

1 detergent molecule

2 grease

3

◄ Detergent molecules clean clothes by surrounding particles of grease and dirt. They lift the dirt off so it can be rinsed away.

diamond

Atoms of CARBON joined in a three dimensional pattern form CRYSTALS of diamond. Diamond is the hardest substance in the world. The only thing that can cut it is another diamond.

diesel

In 1892 Dr Rudolf Diesel, a German engineer, designed an INTERNAL COMBUSTION ENGINE that could run on COAL dust (CARBON). Later, the design was changed so that the engine could run on heavy OIL instead. There is no spark plug in a diesel engine. Instead, the fuel heats up as it is compressed and explodes by itself, driving the pistons up and down.

▼ In a diesel engine, the up–down motion of the pistons is changed into the rotating motion of the crankshaft which drives the wheels.

digital

Digital systems turn information into BINARY code. A sound RECORDING may store digitized information. Each digital value says how loud, or how high a note might

▲ Fresh water can be distilled from boiling salt water. The salt is left behind as the water evaporates. The water vapour is cooled in a condenser, and pure water drips into a flask.

be. From this a whole orchestral concert can be played back. The quality of digital recordings is very high. The pattern of dots you can see in a newspaper photograph shows a digitized image.

distillation

Distillation is used to separate a liquid from another substance. DESALINATION uses distillation. The process is also used to separate ALCOHOL from WATER. Ethanol (alcohol) boils at a lower temperature than water. So, when the mixture is heated, the alcohol EVAPORATES first and can be cooled and collected.

Doppler effect

Sound WAVES travel at speed from their source. If the source is moving towards you, the SOUND waves are pushed together and the frequency of the note goes up. When the source is moving away from you, the sound waves are farther apart. You can hear this when an ambulance goes past with its siren on. The note is higher as it approaches, and lower as the

frequency increases

frequency decreases

sound waves

◀ Sound waves are squashed up in front of an ambulance, so the siren sounds higher as it travels towards you.

ambulance is speeding away. This is called the Doppler effect, in memory of the German scientist Johann C. Doppler, who first explained it.

drug

Drugs are CHEMICALS which alter the body. Some, such as aspirin, are used to control pain. Antibiotics help the body to fight infections. Some drugs are used to alter peoples' mood. CAFFEINE, NICOTINE and ALCOHOL are all drugs. Many drugs have dangerous side-effects, and some are very addictive.

▶ Plants are the source of many modern medicines. The drugs digitalin and digoxin can be obtained from the dried leaves of the foxglove plant. These drugs are used to treat heart failure. The foxglove is called *Digitalis*, because its flowers fit on your fingers (digits)!

foxglove

DID YOU KNOW?

Many important drugs were found in plants. Many of them have been used for hundreds of years by ancient tribes. The Madagascar periwinkle provides two drugs that are used to treat cancer. Curare, used to relax patients during major surgery, was used on poison darts by Amazon indians. And the liquorice plant has given us a new drug for the treatment of stomach ulcers! Aspirin was discovered in willow trees. The bark was used for centuries to treat people with fever, which we use aspirin for today.

dye

A dye alters the colour of an object. Old-fashioned dyes often come from strange places. Cochineal (red food colour) comes from crushed insects. Chemical dyes are used to colour CLOTH. Older dyes used to wash out from the cloth. But many modern dyes fix so powerfully to the fibres that they almost never fade.

dynamo

A dynamo is a device that turns mechanical motion into ELECTRICITY. See **generator**.

E

Earth see **Solar System**

earthquake

When rock masses slip against each other they vibrate. These vibrations can spread over vast distances. This is an earthquake. There are about 10,000 earthquakes felt each year. Most are

▼ Many modern buildings, especially in areas where earthquakes can be expected, are built to withstand the shock of an earthquake, but older buildings collapse more easily.

small, but there is a large tremor somewhere every week. Earthquakes usually occur in places where the moving plates on the Earth's crust rub together. The most famous earthquake zone is in California, USA, along the San Andreas fault. See **plate tectonics**.

echo

SOUND waves can bounce back from a solid surface. You hear the sound a second time a little later and more faintly. This is an echo. See **sonar**.

eclipse

The SUN is much larger than the MOON. But because the Moon is nearer to Earth, both seem about the same size in the sky. Sometimes the Moon passes between us and the Sun. When this happens, the Moon blocks the Sun out. This is a solar eclipse. Some nights the Moon passes

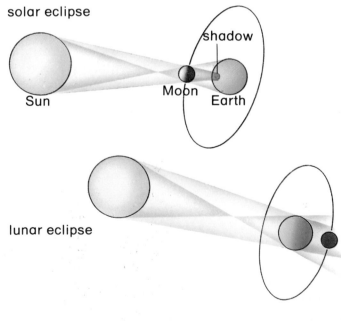

solar eclipse

Sun   Moon   shadow   Earth

lunar eclipse

▲ The Moon disappears in the Earth's shadow during a lunar eclipse. The solar eclipse occurs when the Moon passes between the Earth and Sun, and blots out the Sun for several minutes.

through the Earth's own shadow. When this happens the Sun can no longer shine on the Moon. The result is an eclipse of the Moon.

LIFE STORY

Edison

Thomas Alva Edison was born in 1847 in the United States. He became one of the greatest scientific inventors. Communications fascinated him, and he set up a telegraph business, wiring messages across America. He worked on electric lights, the typewriter, methods of duplicating documents, and many other ideas. Edison did not always invent things. Often he took an invention, and improved it. One of these was the telephone. This led him to invent the gramophone, which could record the human voice for the first time.

Edison's phonograph

electricity see **pages 42 and 43**

electromagnetism

Electromagnetism is the study of magnets and electric currents. An electromagnet is made with a core of iron and a wire coil wrapped around it. When an electric current flows in the coil, the iron becomes

a magnet. Beams of electrons in the cathode ray tube of a TV set can be focused onto the screen with magnetic fields, using an electromagnetic lens. Geologists even use electromagnets to find metal ores under the ground. This is called electromagnetic prospecting.

switch

+ −

insulated wire

▲ You can make an electromagnet by wrapping a wire around an iron nail and connecting it to a battery. Try using it to pick up small nails.

electron

An electron is a tiny particle in an ATOM. Each electron has a single negative ELECTRIC charge. Beams of electrons are sometimes called CATHODE RAYS.

electron microscope

An ELECTRON microscope uses beams of electrons to produce a magnified view of a specimen. It produces a far more detailed image than a light MICROSCOPE, but cannot be used to study living things as a light microsope can. The electron beams are focused with ELECTROMAGNETIC lenses. In a scanning electron microscope we look at the electrons reflected from a solid specimen. This gives a three-dimensional view, so CRYSTALS, insects and other solid specimens look very vivid in the scanning electron microscope.

ELECTRICITY

Electricity is the result of electrons moving about. If they collect in one place, static electricity builds up. But if they move along, an electric current is produced. People sometimes mistakenly speak of electricity as a 'fuel'. Oil, gas and coal are fuels, but electricity is a form of energy. It can be produced by a generator using any kind of fuel. The electrons are moved about by some outside form of energy.

▼ A magnetic field is created between the poles of a magnet. If the field is cut by a moving wire coil, then electrons will move along the wire. If the wire is part of a circuit, an electric current will flow. This is a simple electric generator. The same effect works in the opposite direction. If you pass a current of electricity through a wire coil in a magnetic field, then the wire will move. An electric motor uses this effect to turn electrical energy into mechanical energy.

▼ Power stations burn fuel to make steam. The steam turns blades in the generator and produces electricity. In order to deliver as much power as possible the electricity is sent out at an extremely high voltage.

▼ Electricity is sent along power cables supported by pylons. The high voltage is very dangerous. But it allows the cables to carry large amounts of electricity without over-heating.

electric generator

poles of magnet

movement of coil

wire coil

current produced in wire

magnetic field

power station

industry (10–30kV)

transformer

pylon

substation

domestic supply (100 or 240V)

◄ Before the electricity is supplied to factories and homes, the voltage must be reduced. This is done at a local sub-station in residential areas and industrial centres. Mains voltage is a thousand times less than in the cross-country cables – but it can still kill.

Mains electricity is used to power many domestic objects: the microwave oven, power-drill, toaster and iron are examples. Torches and portable cassette players can run on batteries.

tape wire to each end of battery

◄ The central rod and outer casing react with the paste inside to produce electricity.

◄ A typical battery produces about two volts of electricity. A torch with a four-volt bulb takes two batteries.

▼ One flash of lightning can have the voltage of 50 million batteries!

carbon rod

hemical paste

insulated wire

zinc casing

electricity flows around circuit and lights bulb

electron

copper atom

◄ Electrons passing from one atom in a wire to the next create a current. The voltage from the battery drives them around the circuit.

◄ Use a torch battery, a small bulb and some lengths of insulated copper wire to build your own circuit. Tape the wire to each end of the battery, and the bulb will light. You could light a toy house like this. Use a paper-clip and two drawings pins for a switch.

▶ You can make your own electroplating bath by dipping two spoons in a copper sulphate solution and connecting them to a battery. The electric current flows through the solution, carrying particles of copper onto the spoon connected to the battery's negative terminal. This spoon turns reddish as it is plated with copper.

electroplating

Some metals, such as CHROMIUM and SILVER, are very useful for coating others. Elecroplating uses an electric current to carry ions of the METAL on to the object to be coated. Metal objects are often electroplated to protect them from CORROSION.

element

There are 109 known elements. These are the basic ATOMS from which COMPOUNDS are made. All the atoms in an element are the same. Each element has a chemical symbol. OXYGEN is O, NITROGEN is N and HYDROGEN is H. Au is the symbol for gold, from the Latin word *aurum*. The elements are listed in the periodic table according to the number of protons they contain. Hydrogen, number one, has one PROTON in its nucleus, helium has two. The elements in each column, or group, have much in common. Lithium, SODIUM and POTASSIUM in the first group are all soft, reactive metals.

▶ The periodic table groups the elements into columns. The atomic number (above each symbol) is the number of protons it contains.

energy see **pages 46 and 47**

engine

Engines burn FUEL to release ENERGY. The energy is then used to do work, like turning wheels or driving a propeller. Early engines were powered by wind (windmills) or water (water-wheels). Later, fuels such as coal were burned to heat water and produce steam, to drive powerful steam engines. Engineers then realized that it was even better to burn the fuel inside the engine as the energy could be produced immediately. This is how an INTERNAL COMBUSTION ENGINE works.

alkali metals	inner transition metals	
transition metals	non-metals	

1 Hydrogen H								
1	**2**							
3 Lithium Li	4 Beryllium Be							
11 Sodium Na	12 Magnesium Mg							
19 Potassium K	20 Calcium Ca	21 Scandium Sc	22 Titanium Ti	23 Vanadium V	24 Chromium Cr	25 Manganese Mn	26 Iron Fe	27 Cobalt Co
37 Rubidium Rb	38 Strontium Sr	39 Yttrium Y	40 Zirconium Zr	41 Niobium Nb	42 Molybdenum Mo	43 Technetium Tc	44 Ruthenium Ru	45 Rhodium Rh
55 Caesium Cs	56 Barium Ba	57–71 Lanthanide series	72 Hafnium Hf	73 Tantalum Ta	74 Tungsten W	75 Rhenium Re	76 Osmium Os	77 Iridium Ir
87 Francium Fr	88 Radium Ra	89–103 Actinide series	Element 104	105 Element 105	106 Element 106	107 Element 107	108 Element 108	109 Element 109

57 Lanthanum La	58 Cerium Ce	59 Praseodym-ium Pr	60 Neodymium Nd	61 Prometheum Pm	62 Samarium Sm	63 Europium Eu	64 Gadolinium Gd	65 Terbium Tb
89 Actinium Ac	90 Thorium Th	91 Protactinium Pa	92 Uranium U	93 Neptunium Np	94 Plutonium Pu	95 Americium Am	96 Curium Cm	97 Berkelium Bk

erosion

Erosion means 'wearing away'. Wind, water and ice can erode solid rock, cutting deep river valleys and shaping the coastline. Wind and rain can cause soil erosion on cultivated land. The topsoil is blown or washed away, leaving bare land where no crops can grow.

escape velocity

A spacecraft has to reach a certain speed to escape the pull of the Earth's GRAVITY. The exact speed is the escape VELOCITY, which is 11.2 kilometres per second.

evaporation

Evaporation is the CHANGE OF STATE from liquid to gas. Evaporation uses up HEAT ENERGY, which is why sweat evaporating from your skin cools you down.

expansion

A metal gets larger when it is heated. This increase in volume or length is known as expansion. Water is unusual because it expands as it freezes, which is why ice can burst pipes.

explosives

The biggest man-made explosions have been made by nuclear weapons. Chemical explosives are high in energy and need HEAT or a physical shock to set them off. Once the reaction starts the heat produced sets off the whole explosion. A vast amount of heat and gas are released with great force. NITROGLYCERINE is a common explosive used to make dynamite. Ammonium nitrate is used in mines. Gunpowder is an explosive used to make FIREWORKS.

groups of elements

	3	4	5	6	7	8
						2 Helium He
	5 Boron B	6 Carbon C	7 Nitrogen N	8 Oxygen O	9 Fluorine F	10 Neon Ne
	13 Aluminium Al	14 Silicon Si	15 Phosphorus P	16 Sulphur S	17 Chlorine Cl	18 Argon Ar
28 Nickel Ni	29 Copper Cu	30 Zinc Zn	31 Gallium Ga	32 Germanium Ge	33 Arsenic As	34 Selenium Se	35 Bromine Br	36 Krypton Kr
46 Palladium Pd	47 Silver Ag	48 Cadmium Cd	49 Indium In	50 Tin Sn	51 Antimony Sb	52 Tellurium Te	53 Iodine I	54 Xenon Xe
78 Platinum Pt	79 Gold Au	80 Mercury Hg	81 Thallium Tl	82 Lead Pb	83 Bismuth Bi	84 Polonium Po	85 Astatine At	86 Radon Rn

66 Dysprosium Dy	67 Holmium Ho	68 Erbium Er	69 Thulium Tm	70 Ytterbium Yb	71 Lutetium Lu
98 Californium Cf	99 Einsteinium Es	100 Fermium Fm	101 Mendelev-ium Md	102 Nobelium No	103 Lawrencium Lr

ENERGY

Energy is everywhere, and is constantly changing from one form to another. The energy from fuels is used in a power station to turn water into steam to make electrical energy. You use the energy in your food to move about and keep warm. The Sun is beaming energy at us too. Energy allows work to be done. The energy of a moving object is called *kinetic energy*. A brick on top of a wall has *potential energy*. This energy was stored in the brick when it was put there in the first place and is released when you push it off the wall. The chemicals in fireworks react together to release the energy that shoots them into the air.

▼ When we burn coal or oil we use stored energy from the sunlight that shone millions of years ago. When the huge coal forests died, they formed such huge piles that there was not enough oxygen for them to rot away, and they turned into coal.

▼ The ancient forest plants stood a hundred metres tall. In the swamps where they grew, the layer of dead plants grew steadily thicker. The solar energy which gave them life was trapped in the huge tree trunks when they died.

▼ The Sun shines light and heat energy on the Earth. Some of this heats the Earth, but much of it bounces back into space. Some is trapped and stored by living things.

▼ The only living things that can trap solar energy as they grow are green plants. Plants use the sunlight to make food out of water and carbon dioxide in their leaves.

▼ Earthworms are an energy-rich food. We do not appreciate them, but chickens and ducks like to eat worms whenever they can.

▼ A chicken sandwich gives you energy to grow. The energy came from the chicken's diet of grain and, of course, those earthworms.

▼ In time, the pressure of new layers of plants and rock turned the plant remains into coal. Huge seams of coal have been found, some deep underground.

▼ Coal is mined from the underground seams. Coal is full of energy and burns easily. The heat can be used to produce steam at a power station.

▼ Some crops produce a kilogram of new growth per square metre in a single season. Plants are used as an energy source by grazing animals such as rabbits, sheep and cows.

▼ Unluckily for rabbits, foxes like to use small animals as their own energy source. The energy that is stored in the rabbit's body then becomes food for the fox.

▼ A dead fox is an ideal food for a scavenger, such as a crow. The rest of the fox's body provides energy for tiny creatures in the soil. The solar energy has now been used four times!

▼ As well as feeding teeming masses of microscopic organisms, decaying animals and plants make the soil a rich source of food for the earthworms. They too become food in time.

▼ The energy from this chain of events is what you use to live, to move, even to throw stones at cans on the top of a wall. It all came from the Sun.

▼ The stone missed! The energy used to throw the stone is transferred to a window, which breaks. The energy chain ends in trouble.

▼ After its long journey, through five kinds of animals (from rabbits to people) the solar energy ends up as the energy which breaks a window and makes the sound of a loud crash!

▼ The steam is used to drive giant turbines. In this way a coal-fired power station turns the solar energy first trapped by the coal forests, into electricity.

▼ Microphones, motors, and even some cars can be powered by electricity. So can burglar alarms. An alarm has been set off by the broken window.

▶ The energy used to throw the stone and break the window set off the alarm. The alarm itself is powered by electricity made from the solar energy stored underground in coal for millions of years.

F

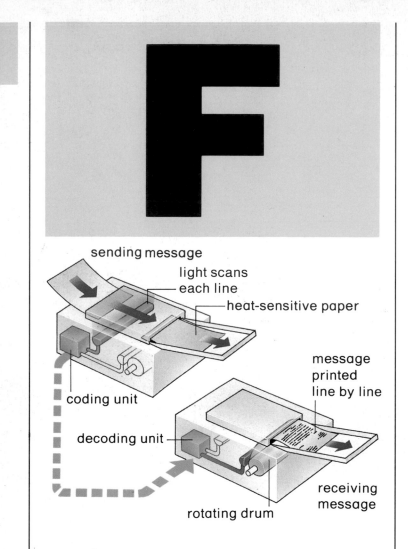

sending message
light scans
each line
heat-sensitive paper

message
printed
line by line

coding unit

decoding unit

receiving
message

rotating drum

▲ A fax machine changes a page of information into a sound code. Another fax machine uses the code to create a copy. The fax sends pictures and text down a telephone line.

fax

Fax is short for facsimile. It is a way of sending images on paper by telephone. A beam of light scans across the images or message on a sheet of paper. The reflected beam is converted into digital signals. These are sent down the wire like a normal telephone transmission. At the other end, the signals are fed to a line of tiny metal probes. These get hot where the signal indicates 'black' and cold when the signal means 'white'. A roll of heat-sensitive paper passes across the line of probes. Where it is heated it turns black. Otherwise it stays white. In this way the whole image is built up, line by line.

feedback

Feedback is the way that an action can be controlled by the result it causes. For example, a machine that goes too fast can automatically cut off its own electricity supply, preventing it going any faster. An early feedback device was the governor of a STEAM engine. If the engine went too fast, spinning metal spheres would swing out and cut off the steam supply so the engine slowed down.

fibres

Fibres are fine threads. Natural fibres are obtained from animals and plants. Synthetic fibres include NYLON. They are made from by-products of the PLASTICS industry. Clothes made with synthetics dry more quickly than natural fibres.

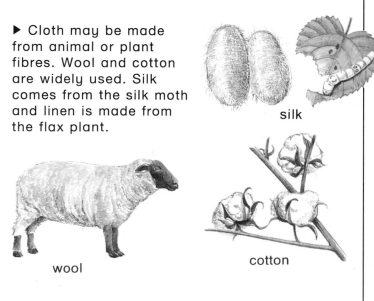

▶ Cloth may be made from animal or plant fibres. Wool and cotton are widely used. Silk comes from the silk moth and linen is made from the flax plant.

silk

wool

cotton

film see **photography**

fire see **combustion**

FIREWORKS

Fireworks are cardboard tubes filled with gunpowder. A chemical inside gives out oxygen when it is heated. This lets the charge burn, even though it is shut away inside a tube, out of contact with the air. Different chemicals are used for different effects and colours. They might create flower shapes that burst in the air, or flashes of brilliant light. The technical term for the study of fireworks is pyrotechnics. Fireworks can be very dangerous and must be handled with care.

wood cap

paper cap

chemicals for stars

gunpowder fuel

Gunpowder fuels the rocket. The chemicals produce different colours. Strontium produces bright red, sodium, yellow and barium, green.

▲ Nuclear fission can be controlled to generate electricity. In a nuclear bomb the chain reaction accelerates uncontrollably due to the amount of uranium present, causing a violent explosion.

fission

Some heavy ATOMS are unstable. They can be broken in two. When this happens NEUTRONS are shot out as the nucleus splits open, releasing a large amount of nuclear ENERGY. Each of these neutrons will in turn split any atom it hits. This gives out still more neutrons, and they split many more atoms. Once this happens, all the atoms start to undergo fission. This is a chain reaction. As the atomic nuclei break up, a large amount of energy is released. This can be used to cause an explosion or, if controlled, to generate NUCLEAR POWER.

flame

A flame is the hot, glowing gas formed during COMBUSTION.

flight

Like birds, aircraft have curved wings. This enables them to produce enough lift for flight. Air rushing over the curved top of the wings has to flow faster than the air below as it has farther to travel. The air pressure below the wing is greater than that above, and this produces lift. Lift must be greater than the force of GRAVITY acting on the plane's weight. Forward thrust is provided by the ENGINES.

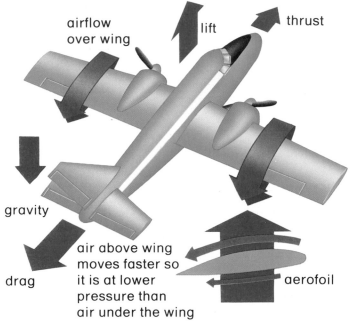

airflow over wing   lift   thrust

gravity

air above wing moves faster so it is at lower pressure than air under the wing

drag   aerofoil

▲▼ Four forces act on a bird or an aircraft in flight. The wings create lift, while the weight of the body pulls down. Engines (or bird wings) create thrust, while air resistance causes drag.

▲ The flywheel is so heavy it spins at a steady speed. This keeps the engine running smoothly.

flywheel

A flywheel is a heavy wheel. Once it is spinning round, it will keep spinning until something stops it. This is because it has INERTIA. Without a flywheel a car engine would run roughly, because INTERNAL COMBUSTION engines have a series of EXPLOSIONS going on inside. But the heavy flywheel in the engine absorbs the irregularities and keeps the engine turning smoothly. See **gyroscope**.

fog

Fog is a greyish cloud which stops you seeing very far. It is an AEROSOL of tiny droplets of water in the AIR close to the ground. If you can see quite far, it is called a mist. When a fog is combined

▼ A warm wind blowing over cold water collects vapour from the water. When the moist wind meets the land, it cools and the vapour it carries changes back into water droplets. This is fog.

with smoke particles it may be called smog. Photochemical smog forms when sunlight acts on traffic and factory fumes in cities. See **pollution**.

force

Any kind of action that makes an object start moving, or changes the way it moves, is a force. Your hand pushing, like the wind blowing, is a force.

forensics

Science can be used to solve crime. Evidence is gathered from the scene of the crime and is analysed by forensic scientists. They can look at fingerprints under a MICROSCOPE and identify a suspect because everyone's fingerprints are unique. Or some grains of pollen found on clothing may prove what the wearer was doing. Chemical tests can identify explosives. Even the smallest piece of matter can usually be identified by a forensic scientist and may provide clues to what happened.

▼ A criminal may be identified by matching a fingerprint found at the scene of a crime.

formula

A formula is a recipe, and shows the make-up of a chemical COMPOUND. The symbols for the ELEMENTS are used with numbers to show how they are combined. How does carbon burn with oxygen? With a formula it is easy to see. The carbon is C, and oxygen is O. Write this out and we see that carbon burns to form carbon monoxide then with more oxygen the carbon monoxide burns to make carbon dioxide:

$$C + O = CO$$
$$CO + O = CO_2$$

fossil

Fossils are the remains of plants and animals from millions of years ago. They were buried in mud or silt after they died. In time, the hard parts, like bones or the veins of leaves, turned to stone and these we know as fossils. The soft parts just rot away but we can often see the impression they left behind in the rock.

▼ Millions of years ago the remains of plants and dead animals were covered with mud and turned into stone. The fossils are found when the rocks above them are eroded away.

fossil fuels

Some fossilized plant remains can burn. Examples are coal and oil. Coal is fossilized trees, and oil is formed from tiny plants and animals that lived in the sea millions of years ago. Because these are the remains of early forms of life, we call them fossil fuels. See **fossil**.

LIFE STORY

Foucault

Jean Bernard León Foucault was a French scientist who invented the GYROSCOPE. In 1851 he set up an experiment to show that the Earth rotates. He hung up a long PENDULUM in Paris and set it swinging. He marked the position on the ground when it started to swing. As hours went by, the pendulum moved from the mark. In fact, it was still swinging in the same direction – it was the Earth which had turned.

weight

time in hours

freeze drying

Freeze drying is a way of preserving food. If frozen food is placed in a VACUUM, the ICE will then sublime away – it will evaporate without melting. The food is left in its original state but bone dry and permanently preserved.

freezing

Freezing is when a liquid becomes solid as it cools. WATER freezes to ICE at a temperature of 0°C (273 K).

friction

Friction is the force that stops surfaces sliding easily against each other. If you slide your hand across a brick wall, for example, there is high friction. But wet soap in the shower slips around with low friction. A LUBRICANT, like oil, can help to reduce friction in machinery. But the soles of your shoes are designed to have high friction. You need friction to walk safely. If you have ever walked on smooth ICE (which has very low friction) you'll know how important friction can be.

▼ Bicycle brakes work by friction. When the rider squeezes the brake lever, a pair of brake blocks are pressed against the wheel. The grip steals energy from the wheel and slows it down.

brake blocks

tyre

fuel

Fuels are substances which burn to give out HEAT ENERGY. Coal, wood and alcohol can be used as fuels. Energy can also be obtained without actual burning taking place. In a fuel cell, HYDROGEN and OXYGEN will react without ever producing a FLAME. The ATOMS join to form MOLECULES of WATER, and ELECTRICITY is produced. Fuel injection is a system of squirting fuel into an ENGINE, to produce extra POWER.

fuse

Fusing means melting. A fuse is a piece of wire in a CIRCUIT that melts if the CURRENT is too strong. See **circuit breaker**.

▶ Electric current flows through a fuse wire unless the current is greater than a certain value. If the current is larger than this, the fuse wire heats up and melts, or 'blows', and the circuit is broken.

fusion

Nuclear FISSION releases ENERGY when heavy atomic nuclei split. But energy is also released when light nuclei join to form bigger ones. This is fusion power. When atoms of heavy ISOTOPES of HYDROGEN react together they join to form HELIUM, and energy is released. This is the reaction that takes place in the SUN. It has been used to make the HYDROGEN BOMB.

To harness fusion power, you need to use a powerful reactor. In 1991, the Joint European Torus (JET) produced some fusion energy for the first time in history. One day we may be able to use this idea to make ELECTRICITY. See **nuclear power**.

G

galaxy

A galaxy is a collection of stars. There are about a hundred million galaxies in the universe. If you look at the night sky, many of the 'stars' you see are actually galaxies. And each galaxy contains millions of stars.

galvanizing

Galvanizing is the process of coating steel with zinc. This delays CORROSION.

gasoline

Gasoline is a fuel that is distilled from crude OIL. See **petrochemicals**.

gas turbine

Normal TURBINES spin round when they are driven. A gas turbine spins by using energy that it releases inside itself. The best example of a gas turbine is a jet engine. Gas turbines are used in planes and power stations, and have been used in experimental cars.

Geiger counter

The most common apparatus for measuring NUCLEAR RADIATION is a Geiger counter. It converts radiation into pulses of electricity which can be heard as clicks on a loudspeaker.

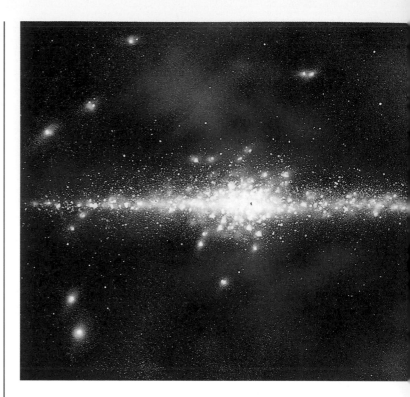

▲ Viewed edge-on, a spiral galaxy is a flat disc of stars with a bulge at its middle. Seen from above, its spiral arms snake out into space.

gem

Gems are MINERALS which look beautiful. The most costly is DIAMOND, the hardest mineral in the world. Other gems include sapphire, ruby, opal and emerald. Some have practical uses, for example ruby can be used to make LASERS.

emerald

sapphire

diamond

▲ When gems are mined, they are usually irregular lumps of dull crystal. They are transformed into sparkling precious stones by cutting and polishing.

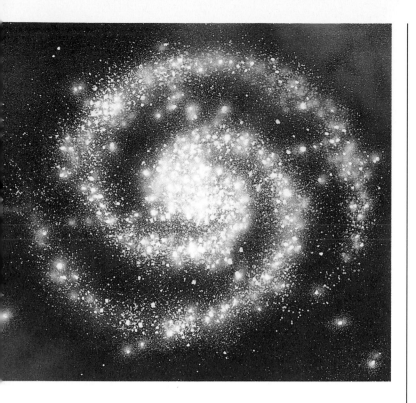

geography
Geo- is Greek for the Earth, and *graphikos* means drawing. So geography is the recording of the Earth's surface.

geology
Geology is the study of the rocks and minerals in the Earth's crust, and the processes that have shaped the land.

▼ Geologists study the Earth's rocks. Rocks are formed when lava hardens, and when layers of rocks or sediments are heated or compressed.

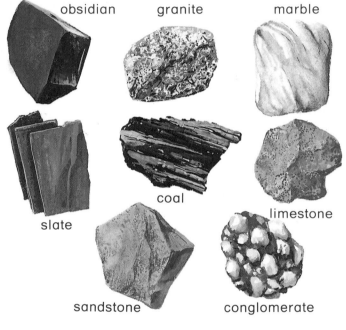

obsidian · granite · marble · slate · coal · limestone · sandstone · conglomerate

geometry
Metrès is Greek for 'measurer'. So geometry started out as the MEASURING of the EARTH. It has moved on to be the measurement of shapes in general. Circles, squares and triangles have been studied for thousands of years, and this is the basis of the part of MATHEMATICS called geometry.

generator
If you turn a wire coil in a MAGNETIC field, then you generate ELECTRICITY. Simple generators are used to power bicycle lamps. In this kind of generator, known as a dynamo, the magnet spins, and the coil stays still.

motion · magnet · wire coil · commutator

▲ An electricity generator works by spinning a coil of wire in a magnetic field. As the wire cuts through the magnetic field, an electric current flows through the coil and, here, lights a bulb.

geothermal
Thermal means 'heat'. So geothermal describes the heat ENERGY inside the EARTH. It can be used as a source of power.

▶ If underground water meets hot rocks and boils suddenly, the result is a geyser – a jet of steam and water gushing out of the ground. Geysers are often found where there are or were volcanoes, such as New Zealand, Iceland and the United States.

geyser
Water deep inside layers of ROCK below ground is sometimes heated by VOLCANIC activity. Then the water boils, and shoots out of cracks, forming a geyser.

glacier
Glaciers form when huge masses of ice build up in mountain valleys. The PRESSURE of the glacier melts the ice underneath, so the whole mass moves downhill at up to 20 metres a day.

▼ As a glacier moves downhill it drags rocks and mud, building up ridges called moraines. Lakes are formed in hollows in the valley.

glass
Glass is a blend of silica (SILICON dioxide), the mineral in sand. Commercial glass is made by melting a mixture of sand with sodium carbonate and a little limestone to help it melt. Glass has no fixed melting point. It simply gets softer as it heats up. While it is hot it can be moulded or blown into shape before it is allowed to cool and set hard.

▶ Gold is an inert metal and will not react with most substances. Gold reflects heat. A thin wrapping of gold protected the Lunar Module from getting too hot.

gold
Gold is a precious yellow metal that has been known for thousands of years. It is not affected by most of the acids and gases which attack other metals. Gold can be hammered so thin that light shines through it. In this form, gold leaf, it is used to cover objects with a thin layer of the metal. Because gold is so valuable it has always been RECYCLED and reused. If you

tributary glacier

fresh snow

ice   pressure   crevasses

moraine

rock

meltwater

have some gold at home it may contain some gold from the Spanish conquest of Mexico, in the 16th century.

governor

A governor is a device for controlling speed. The first governors were on steam engines. They stopped the engine going too fast. See **feedback**.

graph

Often the clearest way to see information in MATHEMATICS is to draw it out on squared paper, or on a COMPUTER. Values are plotted as points on the graph, then joined up to make a curve. A graph shows how one value changes with time, or compared to another value.

▲ A graph showing the speed of a moving object is drawn by plotting the distance travelled against time. The shape of the curve shows how the speed changes.

gravity

Gravity is the force that pulls objects towards the ground. Large amounts of mass pull other masses towards them. The Earth's gravity stops you floating up towards the ceiling. The laws of gravity were said to have been worked out by Isaac Newton, after an apple fell from a tree. He realized that the MOON didn't fall, although it was very heavy. This gave him the idea of gravity pulling downwards, matched by the VELOCITY of the Moon keeping it in ORBIT.

▶ Gravity pulls the Earth and Moon towards each other. The Earth is much larger than the Moon, and its gravitational force is six times as strong.

greenhouse effect see **page 58**

gunpowder

Gunpowder is a mixture of sulphur, saltpetre and charcoal. This EXPLOSIVE was known to the Ancient Chinese, who used it to make FIREWORKS.

gyroscope

Everyone is fascinated by gyroscopes. A gyroscope is a spinning metal FLYWHEEL. A gyroscope will not fall as long as it is spinning fast. The flywheel has MOMENTUM, and always tries to point in the same direction. Gyroscopes are used for navigating on planes and ships. Whatever the direction of travel, the gyroscope will always point the same way.

▶ A spinning gyroscope can be balanced on the tip of a pencil as long as its flywheel is spinning. The gyroscope falls over when the flywheel slows down.

GREENHOUSE EFFECT

Energy shines onto the Earth from the Sun. It is reflected back again as heat, but much of it is trapped by gases in the atmosphere and cannot escape. This greenhouse effect keeps our climate balanced. Not all the gases in the air trap the heat equally. Carbon dioxide traps a large amount of heat. Burning fossil fuels, in cars and power stations, adds to the carbon dioxide in the atmosphere. As a result, more heat is trapped, and the world may be getting warmer.

▶ Half of the global warming is caused by carbon dioxide; 15 percent is caused by methane; 25 percent by CFCs and the rest by nitrogen oxides.

▼ The extra heat trapped by the greenhouse gases may be heating the atmosphere by 1°C every thirty years. This small change in temperature could have dramatic effects on the climate. If the ice and snow melted, the sea could rise and flood a lot of land. The only answer is to cut back on the release of greenhouse gases.

sunlight

some heat escapes from the atmosphere

heat is reflected from the Earth's surface

greenhouse gases trap heat and reflect it back to Earth

Sun's rays heat the Earth

greenhouse gases are produced by factories, power plants, farms and car exhausts

Earth's atmosphere

glass prevents heat escaping

Sun's rays

◀ We call this the 'greenhouse effect' because gases such as carbon dioxide and methane act like the glass in a greenhouse. The layer of glass prevents the Sun's heat from escaping, so the greenhouse stays warm.

half-life

The ATOMS of unstable ISOTOPES break down as time goes by. At first they break down quickly, but as there are fewer and fewer atoms left they break down more slowly. The half-life is the length of time it takes for half of the atoms to break down. For some materials, like plutonium, the half-life is millions of years. But for an isotope of lithium the half-life is less than a billionth of a billionth of a second.

hardness

The hardness of water depends on the amount of lime dissolved in it. The hardness of solids is measured on Mohs' scale. The softest mineral is talc, numbered one on the scale. Talc is so soft it can be scratched with a finger-nail. The hardest mineral is diamond, which is number ten on the scale. Each mineral can scratch the next one down the list, and so on down the scale.

hardware see **computers, software**

heat see **page 60 and 61**

heat exchanger

A heat exchanger is a device for moving heat from one place to another. The 'radiator' of a car cools the engine by exchanging its heat with the cold air blowing over it from the outside.

▼ A car radiator is a heat exchanger. Water carries heat from the engine. Cold air is drawn through the radiator to cool the water again.

heat pump

A heat pump is like a REFRIGERATOR running in reverse. A heat pump collects the low level of heat in a river, or in the soil and takes it through a series of pipes. The fluid in the pipes is compressed to release the heat. In this way a nearby river can be used to heat a house.

▼ Mohs' scale is used to measure hardness. Materials are compared to ten minerals. A material that scratches apatite but is scratched by orthoclase has a hardness rating of $5\frac{1}{2}$.

MOHS' SCALE

1. talc
2. gypsum
3. calcite
4. fluorite
5. apatite
6. orthoclase
7. quartz
8. topaz
9. corundum
10. diamond

H

HEAT

Heat is a form of energy. It spreads in three ways. One is by slowly spreading through a substance, like warmth along a spoon-handle. This is *conduction*. A second is *convection*, which occurs when a hot liquid expands and rises. Colder liquid takes its place, and (after being heated) rises in its turn, forming a convection current. The third is *radiation*. Radiation is in the form of infrared rays shining across a space. It is how the energy from the Sun reaches us on Earth across the empty space that lies between.

▼ When you heat a saucepan of water, the metal pan is heated by conduction. Then the water inside is heated by convection currents.

convection currents

TEMPERATURE

Temperature tells you how hot something is, but not how much heat it contains. Two objects could be the same temperature but the one that stays hot longer has more heat energy. The lowest temperature possible is absolute zero (−273.16°C) when no heat is present. Even outer space is warmer than this. The nearest anyone has come to absolute zero is two billionths of a degree above it.

▶ Here, one person is feeling heat radiated from the Sun. The other feels it radiated from the heater. Their backs heat up, too. Heat radiating between the two of them causes 'local heating'.

DID YOU KNOW?

As a substance is heated, the atoms or molecules of which it is made become more agitated. They jiggle about more as the temperature goes higher. The top picture of the three shows them totally still. This would be absolute zero. The middle picture shows them as they might be when at room temperature. And the lowest picture shows them jiggling furiously, when very hot.

absolute zero

room temperature

hot

▼ Local heating takes place where two radiating bodies face each other closely. On an electric heater the hottest loops in the coil are those closest together. You may notice that the hottest places in a coal or wood fire are in between the lumps of fuel. This is because the pieces of fuel reflect heat to each other, and the temperature builds up in between. An example of local heating is in a barbecue fire. The hot spots are between the coals. Move them apart and the fire soon dies.

electric fire

coal fire

charcoal fire

The temperature that something reaches depends on how much infrared energy it absorbs. Infrared is reflected from a white surface, and absorbed by a dark one. Try this experiment one sunny day. Stand with one bare foot on a white tile, and the other on one that is black. The white tile will feel much cooler.

▼ Chemical reactions take place more rapidly in hot water than in cold. Dissolve two fizzy tablets, one in hot water, one in cold and you can see which one reacts quickest.

cold water

hot water

H

heavy water

A MOLECULE of normal WATER is made of two ATOMS of HYDROGEN and one of OXYGEN to make the COMPOUND H$_2$O. Heavy water has an unusual hydrogen atom with a neutron in the nucleus. It is also known as deuterium oxide, abbreviated D$_2$O. Heavy water is used in NUCLEAR reactors.

helicopter

A helicopter is an AIRCRAFT in which lift is produced by a large propeller on the top. This propellor is known as the rotor, and it takes the place of wings. It allows the helicopter to take off vertically, and hover in the air, as lift can be produced without the helicopter travelling forwards.

detected by analysing the LIGHT of the SUN before it was known on Earth. Since it does not burn, one of its many uses is in gas-filled BALLOONS and airships.

hertz

ELECTROMAGNETIC WAVES (such as RADIO waves) were discovered by the German physicist Heinrich Hertz who lived from 1857 to 1894. The SI UNIT which measures the frequency of WAVES is hertz (Hz) which is named after him. One vibration or cycle per second equals 1 Hz. The kilohertz is equal to 1000 cycles per second.

◄ A helicopter can be controlled very precisely in all directions by careful use of its overhead main rotor and tail rotor. Its speed and direction is controlled by changing the angle and speed of the rotor blades.

helium

HYDROGEN is the simplest atom of all, with a single proton in the nucleus. Helium is next, with two protons and two neutrons. Its symbol is He. Helium is the second lightest gas (after hydrogen). It was

hologram

A hologram is a recording of the pattern formed when laser light is reflected from an object, and 'interferes' with the original laser beam. The result is a three-dimensional image.

▶ One horse can work at a rate of one horsepower. When engines replaced horses, engine power was still measured in horsepower. It was calculated from the size and number of cylinders in the engine. Engine power is now measured more accurately in brake horsepower (bhp) – the power needed to brake the engine. It is measured by a machine called a dynamometer.

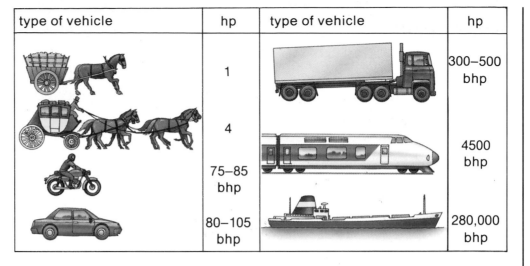

type of vehicle	hp	type of vehicle	hp
	1		300–500 bhp
	4		4500 bhp
	75–85 bhp		280,000 bhp
	80–105 bhp		

horsepower

Horsepower was the power of a single horse. But (since there are strong and weak horses) it is now set at 745.7 WATTS.

hovercraft

A hovercraft is a vehicle that is held above the surface by a cushion of air. Hovercraft can glide straight from land to sea. The first successful hovercraft was designed in England by a boat-builder named Christopher Cockerell in 1955. His first experiments were done with a coffee tin and a hair drier. But earlier, unsuccessful

▼ A hovercraft rides on top of a 'cushion' of air blown beneath the craft by a large fan.

hovercraft had been designed in the United States in 1928, and in Finland in 1930.

humidity

Humidity is a measure of the moisture in the air. When the air cannot hold any more moisture, the humidity is 100 per cent. Hot air can hold more water than cold air. When warm damp air cools, the water condenses to form FOG.

hurricane

A hurricane (or cyclone) is a tropical storm with strong WINDS spinning round a centre of low pressure at up to 125 kilometres per hour.

hydraulics

Hydraulics is the science of how liquids flow. You cannot compress liquids. If you force liquid down one end of a pipe then the same amount of liquid must come out of the other end. You can use this idea to make a foot pedal operate a brake some distance away. A large movement of a small piston is needed to make a large piston move a little way. This is how a hydraulic jack lifts a car.

▲ This is a surface piercing hydrofoil, because the underwater wings are not completely submerged.

hydrofoil

A hydrofoil is a kind of wing that works under water. The word is also used to describe a ship with strong 'wings' underneath. At speed, they make the ship rise out of the water. This cuts down FRICTION and allows the hydrofoil to travel easily across the water.

hydrogen

Hydrogen has the simplest ATOM possible. A hydrogen atom has a single proton in the NUCLEUS and a single ELECTRON in ORBIT around it. This is the lightest ELEMENT in the Universe, and also the most plentiful. See **heavy water, helium**.

hydrogen bomb

At very high levels of energy, hydrogen ISOTOPES can join together to form HELIUM. This reaction gives out large amounts of ENERGY. This is the source of energy inside the SUN. Powerful hydrogen bombs which use this reaction to produce a huge explosion have been tested, but never used in warfare. See **fusion**.

hydrometer

A hydrometer is a device for measuring the DENSITY of a liquid. It is compared to water, which has a density of one.

hydroponics

Hydroponics is growing plants without soil. Instead of rooting plants in soil, hydroponic farmers grow them in water containing all the chemicals that they need. Many commercial crops, such as tomatoes, are grown in this way.

▼ Growing mustard and cress seeds on wet kitchen paper is one form of hydroponics, a method for growing plants without using soil.

hygrometer

A hygrometer is a device for measuring the HUMIDITY of the air. Have you noticed how your hair changes depending on whether the air is wet or dry? Scientists know this too – which is why there is usually a hair inside a hygrometer.

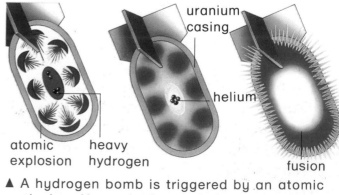

uranium casing

helium

atomic explosion heavy hydrogen

fusion

▲ A hydrogen bomb is triggered by an atomic explosion. Heavy hydrogen atoms are forced together, forming helium and releasing energy.

ice and snow see **page 66**

implosion

An implosion is the opposite of an EXPLOSION. An implosion occurs when something collapses inwards.

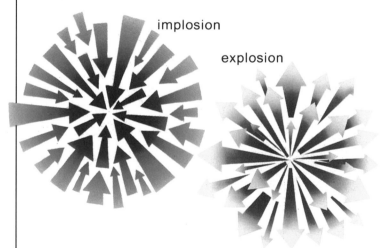

▲ The force of an implosion is directed in towards a central point. Compare this with an explosion, in which the energy bursts outwards.

indicator

An indicator is a chemical whose colour is changed by ACIDS AND ALKALIS. LITMUS is the best known indicator. In an alkali it is blue and in an acid it turns red. In pure water, which is neutral, it is purple. Universal indicator is a mixture of different indicators which tells you exactly how acid (or alkaline) something is by the colour it turns the solution. This

is measured on the pH scale. pH 0 is very acidic, pH 7 neutral, and pH 14 is very strongly alkaline.

1
2 strong acid (hydrochloric acid)
3
4 weak acid (vinegar)
5
6
7 neutral (water)
8
9
10
11 weak alkali (sodium bicarbonate)
12
13
14 sodium hydroxide

◄ It can be important to know the pH value of a solution. For example, some plants will only grow in acid soil. If universal indicator is added to a mixture of the soil and water it changes colour. Comparing the result to a colour chart will give you the pH value of the soil.

inertia

An object that is at rest likes to stay that way. It takes ENERGY to make it move. Once moving, it takes energy to make it stop. This tendency to keep doing the same thing is called inertia.

infinity

Infinity goes on for ever. The number of stars in the Universe is limited. So is the number of sand-grains in the world. But infinity never ends. You cannot imagine it, because everything you experience ends somewhere, even the Universe.

information technology

Information technology is the study of methods of handling data. See **computer, fax, telephone**.

infrared

Infrared waves are the electromagnetic wavelengths which lie beyond the red end of the visible spectrum. Heat rays are infrared. See **light, radiation**.

ICE AND SNOW

Ice is an amazing substance. If you freeze a normal liquid, the solid form always sinks. But when water freezes the ice floats. This is because water expands as it freezes, so the ice is lighter than water. Pure water freezes at 0°C, but adding an impurity such as salt lowers the freezing point. This is why salt is put on roads in winter to melt the ice.

▶ If the air is cold enough, water vapour in clouds will crystallize and form snow. The crystal grows around a tiny speck of dust. Snowflakes are made up of six-sided crystals. Their shape depends on the water vapour, the temperature and many other factors. Each snowflake is unique.

◀ 'Berg' is German for mountain, from which icebergs got their name. Only one-tenth of the iceberg sticks above the surface. The hidden part of an iceberg sank the Titanic.

▼ Skis and skates depend on the fact that ice melts under pressure. As the ice and snow beneath them melts, friction is reduced so they slide easily along.

DID YOU KNOW?

Cold air cannot hold as much water vapour as warm air. As air rises, the vapour may condense to form clouds and rain. But on a cold day snow crystals will form.

When damp air condenses at ground level it forms hoarfrost. You can study the lacy patterns of hoarfrost on a frozen window, or frozen dew on a spider's web using a lens.

▲ Wet washing on a winter clothes-line can freeze solid in minutes. But the ice can still sublime (change directly to water vapour without melting to water first) on a good drying day. So the clothes become soft and 'dry' without the ice melting.

integrated circuit

A large electronic CIRCUIT can be made by putting all the different parts on one tiny silicon wafer. The separate TRANSISTORS, and the wires that join them, are all produced as one. So are all the special items such as resistors (which control the flow of ELECTRICITY) and capacitors (which store it). This is known as an integrated circuit (IC). The central processing unit of a COMPUTER is a special integrated circuit no larger than your finger nail.

internal combustion engine

GAS TURBINES, petrol ENGINES and DIESEL engines all burn their FUEL internally. Burning the fuel produces vast volumes of hot gas, which expand and can be made to do work. In a car it expands in the cylinders and pushes pistons connected to the wheels. In a gas turbine, the gases are compressed by fans and thrust is produced by a jet of escaping waste gases.

air

fuel and air

| induction | compression | combustion | exhaust |

▲ internal combustion engines operate in a 'four stroke' cycle. The piston falls, sucking fuel and air into the cylinder. As it rises, the mixture is compressed and then ignited. The explosion drives the piston down, and it rises again to push out the exhaust gases.

inventions see **page 68**

iodine

Iodine is an ELEMENT with the symbol I. It is a glistening solid which looks like a metal. Iodine dissolves in ALCOHOL to make an antiseptic. It turns starch blue, and can be used as a test for starch (try some on a potato).

ion

An ion is an ATOM which has gained or lost one or more electrons. It is the same as a normal atom, but it will energetically join with other ions that can make up or accept the extra electron(s).

▶ A fluorine atom has nine electrons orbiting the nucleus in two layers, or shells. The outer shell contains seven electrons. If an extra electron joins it, the atom becomes an ion.

fluorine atom

extra electron

fluorine ion

ionosphere

High in the atmosphere, the atoms are so thinly spread out that many of them break into IONS because of the SOLAR ENERGY. This layer is the ionosphere.

iridescence

Iridescence is the name given to the shimmering rainbow effect that can sometimes be seen in bubbles, or in oil on water. It occurs because the LIGHT reflected from the bottom of the oil film interferes with the light bouncing off the top edge of the film. The white light is split into the COLOURS of the rainbow. Some natural objects such as the gemstone opal, and the wings of a butterfly are iridescent. They have patterns of very fine lines which reflect different colours of light. It is strange to think that the brilliant purple of a butterfly's wing is produced by scales that are really brown.

INVENTIONS

Do you know the difference between a discovery and an invention? Discoveries are when people find out about something that already exists – such as gravity, or a drug in a wild plant. An invention is something that people make for the first time. The wheel was an important invention 5000 years ago. Computers are inventions of more recent times.

DID YOU KNOW?

The microchip is one of the smallest inventions. It also has the most uses. These tiny chips control many other inventions – from a huge aircraft to a toaster.

▶ Many inventions of the modern world were developed by individuals working at home. The jet engine was first designed by an engineer in his spare time. The hovercraft was designed by a boat builder as a hobby. Bicycles were invented by a Scottish farmer in 1839. The pneumatic tyre was invented by a vet named J.B. Dunlop, and two Hungarians, Ladislao and Georg Biro, a writer and a chemist, invented the ball-point pen in 1938.

DID YOU KNOW?

John Baird is said to have invented TV, but Ferdinand Braun, a German scientist, had the idea for a television tube in 1897, and Philo Farnsworth built a TV set in the US in 1927.

INVENTIONS TIMETABLE

1,000,000 years ago – stone tools (Hungary)
40,000 BC – bows and arrows (Africa)
10,000 BC – clay pots (Egypt)
8000 BC – copper knives (Iran)
3500 BC – plough (Syria)
3000 BC – wheel (Iraq)
2500 BC – paper, from papyrus reed (Egypt)
2000 BC – kite (China)
1500 BC – sundial (Persia)
1000 BC – iron weapons (Europe)
AD 100 – paper, from pulp (China)
1100 – compass (China)
1440 – printing press (Germany)
1530 – telescope (Italy)
1765 – steam-engine (Britain)
1822 – camera (France)
1835 – computer (Britain)
1903 – aeroplane (United States)
1905 – bakelite (United States)
1920 – helicopter (Spain)
1934 – jet engine (Britain, Germany)
1948 – phototypesetting (France)
1960 – laser (United States)
1958 – silicon chip (United States)
1981 – space shuttle (United States)

▶ Iron is extracted from naturally occurring iron ore in a blast furnace. The ore is burned with limestone and coke. They react with the ore to produce iron which collects as a liquid at the bottom of the furnace. Most of the iron is used to make steel. Steel is iron which contains carbon to make it harder.

iron ore, limestone and coke

hot gases

air heater

blast furnace

dust catcher

hot air

slag

iron

iron

Iron is the most widely used METAL in the world. Wrought iron is hammered out flat, and is used for decorative work. Cast iron is poured into a mould to cool, and is so brittle that it will shatter if you drop it. Iron is also used to make STEEL. Steel is harder than iron, and is used to build bridges, ships and to make cars. Iron and steel react with air and water and form RUST, so they are painted or coated with plastic or zinc to protect them.

irrigation

Irrigation is the piping or raising of water to areas without enough water to grow crops. Farmers have irrigated fields in dry parts of the world for thousands of years.

isobar

Isobars are lines on a WEATHER map that run through areas of equal AIR PRESSURE. Like the contours on a MAP (which show height), isobars show how air pressure changes from one area to another.

high pressure

high pressure

low pressure

low pressure

low pressure

high pressure

◀ The curved lines on this weather map are isobars. They link areas with the same air pressure. The pattern of high and low pressure areas enables scientists to predict the weather in the following day or two. An area of low pressure, such as the one seen here over Europe, brings rainy weather.

69

▲ The isotherms on this map of North America show how the sea helps to keep the land warmer in winter, when cold Arctic air moves south.

isotherm

Isotherms are lines on a climate map that join places with the same temperature. They are used in weather forecasting.

isotope

An ELEMENT has a fixed number of PROTONS in its NUCLEUS. But the number of NEUTRONS may vary. An atom with a different number of neutrons to the most common atom is an isotope. Some isotopes gradually break down, and the rate at which they do this gives the HALF-LIFE.

▼ There are three forms, or isotopes, of hydrogen. Hydrogen has one proton. Deuterium also has a neutron and tritium has two neutrons.

jet see **turbine**

jet stream

The jet stream is a region of strong WIND about 10 kilometres up in the atmosphere. The air-stream may have a speed of about 300 km/h in a band up to 500 kilometres wide. Aircraft can fly faster with the jet stream.

LIFE STORY

Joule

The joule is named after the British physicist James Prescott Joule (1818 – 1889. The joule is a unit of ENERGY. Energy used to be measured in calories. One calorie equals 4.2 joules. Joule studied HEAT and ELECTRICITY. Through his experiments, he showed that when heat is produced, another form of energy is always lost. He therefore proved that heat itself is a form of energy.

Jupiter

Jupiter is the fifth PLANET. Its MASS is 318 times that of Earth. Clouds of frozen chemicals whirl around the surface. Jupiter's red spot is the centre of a CYCLONE which is bigger than the Earth.

kerosene

Kerosene is a liquid FUEL used in many types of INTERNAL COMBUSTION engines. It is also called paraffin.

kilowatt

A kilowatt is an amount of POWER, equal to a thousand WATTS. A kettle rated at one kilowatt would convert 1000 joules of ELECTRICITY into HEAT every second.

kaleidoscope

This simple device was invented in 1816 by Sir David Brewster, a British scientist. A kaleidoscope is a long tube with mirrors set at an angle of 60 degrees. Little pieces of coloured plastic at one end of the kaleidoscope seem to form a continuous star-shaped design because of their REFLECTION. As the tube is turned, the pattern changes endlessly. The pattern may be nothing special. It is the reflections which look amazing.

DID YOU KNOW?

The most powerful nuclear power station in the world is at Fukushima, Japan. Its ten reactors produce 9000 kilowatts (nine megawatts) of power. The largest single reactor is at Ignalina in Lithuania. It produces 1500 megawatts (MW). The most powerful power station of all was built at Grand Coulee, Washington, USA in 1942. Its output is more than 10,000 MW – enough for a city of 16 million people!

▲ You can make your own kaleidoscope by taping three mirrors together, as shown here. Tape a triangle of tracing paper on the end and drop in a few small pieces of coloured paper.

laser see **page 73**

latent heat

Latent means hidden. Latent heat is the ENERGY a substance uses up (or gives out) when it goes through a CHANGE OF STATE. When a solid is heated to its MELTING point, it needs to take in extra HEAT ENERGY to change to a liquid, but its TEMPERATURE stays the same. When the liquid freezes back to a solid, this latent heat is given out again. Latent heat is also taken in when a liquid changes to a gas, and is given out when a gas condenses to a liquid. This is why steam will scald you, and also explains why sweating keeps you cool. Heat from your body is taken in as latent heat, and the drops of sweat evaporate.

latitude and longitude

How do you know where you are on the EARTH'S surface? On land you read a map, or a nearby road sign. But when you are in the middle of the ocean, you have no fixed landmarks. The Earth has only two permanent landmarks, the North and South Poles. Lines of longitude are imaginary lines that run from the North to the South Pole. The place everyone measures from is the Greenwich Meridian. This is the line of 0 longitude which passes through Greenwich in London. Lines of latitude run around the Earth at right angles to longitude. Latitude is measured as degrees North or South of the Equator.

▼ Any place can be identified by its latitude and longitude. New York is at 40°N 74°W, where a line 40 degrees north of the equator crosses another 74 degrees west of Greenwich.

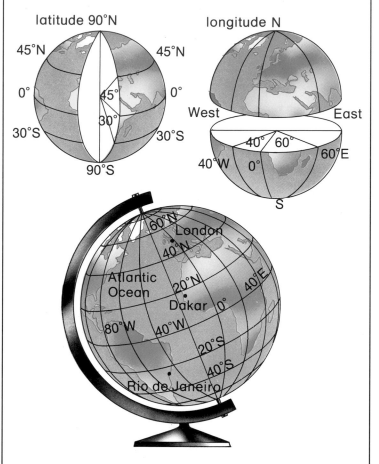

lava

Lava is hot, molten rock from inside the EARTH that is released when a VOLCANO erupts. It is able to flow when red-hot, but slowly hardens as it cools back to rock. Some lava is full of gas bubbles and can actually float! Pumice stone is a kind of lava you can buy at a chemist's shop. The longest lava flow ever recorded measured more than 60 kilometres, in Iceland during 1783.

LASER

Laser stands for: Light Amplification by Stimulated Emission of Radiation. Lasers are a type of maser (these produce microwaves, rather than light). Lasers produce a beam of radiation by pumping energy into atoms, like the atoms in a ruby crystal. As the atoms return to their normal state, the energy is released as an intense beam of pure light.

▼ Light from an ordinary torch is a mixture of different wavelengths, and contains all the colours of the spectrum. The beam spreads out as it leaves the torch.

ordinary light

laser light

▲ Unlike torchlight, laser light is coherent, which means it is all the same wavelength and is in perfect 'step'. Ruby lasers produce flashes, or pulses, of light. Gas lasers produce a continuous beam of laser light from a tube filled with gas.

▶ Lasers can be used in industry. As the laser beam hits a metal surface, the high temperatures produced allow technicians to cut solid steel. Since there is no actual 'blade', it is easier to control the shape of the cut.

▼ Laser light is a powerful form of energy. Eye surgeons use lasers to weld the inside of the eye. The minute weld produced helps the delicate eye tissues hold together while they heal.

▼ The beam of light from a laser does not spread out, like light from a normal lamp. This means it can be used as a perfectly straight line, instead of a ruler. Builders use a laser beam to check if a long tunnel is straight. Tunnels can be bored with amazing accuracy, using a laser to help check the progress.

lead

Lead is a metal. It is soft, heavy and has a low melting point. Its chemical symbol is Pb (from the Latin *plumbum*; a 'plumber' was a person who fitted lead pipes).

lens

Lenses focus rays. If a lens brings the rays closer together it is positive (convex). A negative (concave) lens spreads rays out. Most lenses are made of glass. A positive or convex lens is thicker in the middle and a negative or concave lens is thicker at the edge. You can use a lens to focus an image of a window on the opposite wall, or on a piece of paper. Magnetic lenses can focus beams of ELECTRONS. They are used in ELECTRON MICROSCOPES and TV sets.

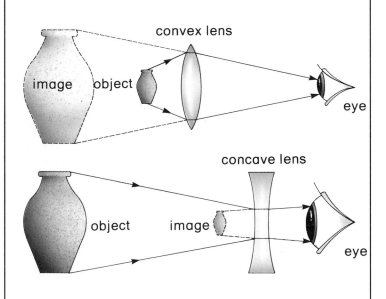

▲ A convex lens bends light rays outwards, so it produces a large image that appears further away. A concave lens bends light rays inwards, producing a small image nearer your eye.

lever

Levers are the simplest of MACHINES. Levers allow you to lift heavy weights more easily. Imagine a strong bar with a weight on one end and someone standing at the other. This is a basic lever. Between the two is the place where the lever turns, called the fulcrum. If the fulcrum is near the weight, little downward PRESSURE, or effort is needed to lift the weight, or load. If the fulcrum is further away, it takes more effort for the person to lift the weight, but they can lift it higher.

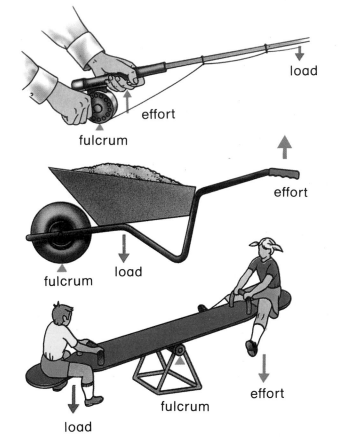

▲ There are three 'classes' of levers. They differ in the positions of the effort, fulcrum and load. A see-saw is a first class lever, a wheelbarrow, second class, and a fishing rod, third class.

light

Light is the very narrow band of ELECTROMAGNETIC RADIATION which we can see. We can see objects only because light is reflected from the object into our eyes and can be focused by a lens. See **colour**.

lightning see **page 76**

LIGHTING

The earliest lamps were oil lamps. As the oil burned, the flame gave out light. Modern lights are powered by electricity. Lights are not just used to help people see around them. Some are used to make light-shows in discos and theatres. Many kinds of lights are used to make brightly coloured advertising signs. Most lights work by heating a metal filament inside the bulb until it glows brightly. Filament lights get hot. Fluorescent lights give out cold light, and use less power.

▶ Standard electric light bulbs have a coiled filament made of tungsten. The filament becomes white-hot in a fraction of a second when the light is turned on. The bulb is filled with an unreactive gas like argon to stop the filament burning away.

◀ Fluorescent lights were usually made as long straight tubes for use in factories or offices, but smaller bulbs are now available. They can be used in a standard light fitting at home. They take a few moments to reach full brightness, but they last far longer and use much less energy than ordinary filament light bulbs.

DID YOU KNOW?

The first electric lamp was made in 1860 by Joseph Swan. He and Thomas Edison later made a lamp with a carbon filament called an 'ediswan' lamp!

inert gas

filament

glass support

electrical contacts

brass cap

◀ At the centre of the light bulb is a glass column. The air is sucked out and replaced with argon.

◀ A fuse is built into the lamp wiring. This melts when the filament eventually burns out and prevents a loud 'bang'.

DID YOU KNOW?

Fluorescent lights have no filament. They contain a gas which glows when electricity passes through it. The gas may give off coloured light. Neon, glows bright red.

LIGHTNING

L

When objects move close to each other they can sometimes transfer electrons. The result is a build-up of static electricity. The most dramatic example is lightning. Massive air currents are caused as hot air rises, often in summer. Droplets of water rise and fall in the rushing currents of air, producing huge charges of static electricity in the clouds. Eventually a massive spark flashes down to Earth, or across to another cloud. The roar of thunder is heard several kilometres away.

▼ Lightning flashes can be 30 kilometres from end to end. The central spark measures no more than two centimetres but the whole glowing flash may be five metres across. The lightning travels at 1500 km/s.

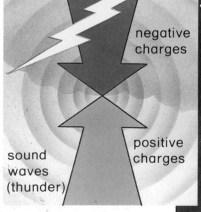

negative charges

positive charges

sound waves (thunder)

▲ Lightning produces about 100 million volts of electricity, and heats the air to over 30,000°C. The rapid expansion of the heated air causes thunder.

DID YOU KNOW?

You can produce miniature 'lightning' at home. Brushing long hair can cause a build-up of static. The crackling sounds are 'thunder'. In a dark room, you can even see the tiny blue sparks of electricity when you take off a synthetic jumper at night. But don't worry, the sparks are harmless.

◄ Philosophers studied lightning for centuries. But the first scientist to investigate it was Benjamin Franklin. He was born in Boston, Massachusetts, USA, in 1706. He became one of America's greatest scientists. In 1746 he tried a very dangerous experiment – he flew a kite into a thundercloud and drew down an electrical charge onto a key. He found he could charge up a leyden jar (an early battery) and store electricity.

light year
A light year is not a time, but a distance. It is the distance that light travels in one year (about 9.5 trillion kilometres).

liquid crystal see page 78

litmus
Litmus is an INDICATOR obtained from the lichen plant *Lecanora*. ACIDS turn litmus red and alkalis turn it blue.

logic
Logic is a system for analysing arguments based on the soundness of earlier statements. Logic is also a way of handling data by COMPUTERS.

▼ A computer breaks down logic operations into a series of simple yes/no questions. This flowchart shows how the decisions a bus driver makes can be broken down in the same way.

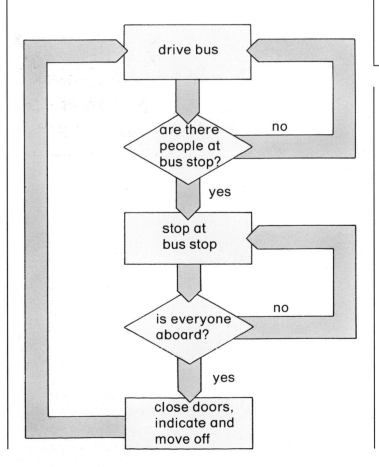

loudspeaker
A loudspeaker changes an electric current into sound. Inside a loudspeaker is a cone. It was traditionally made from paper, but it is now often made of plastic instead. In the middle of the cone is a wire coil around a magnet. This vibrates when an electric current passes through the wire. The current increases and decreases according to the signal received from the radio, television or hi-fi system. As a result, the cone creates an exact copy of the original sound, sending out vibrations which our ears hear as sound.

DID YOU KNOW?
Some hi-fis have several speakers, to reproduce sounds of different frequencies. The result is a higher quality sound than a single speaker could produce. The *tweeter* produces high-pitched sounds and the *squawker* produces sounds in the middle of the range. Low-pitched sounds are produced by the *woofer*.

lubricant
When two materials rub together they produce FRICTION. Oiling the surfaces can help them slide smoothly, because oil is a lubricant. Graphite, a form of CARBON, and talc are solid lubricants.

◄ When surfaces rub together, microscopic roughnesses catch on each other and produce friction.

► A lubricant keeps the surfaces apart so that they can slide more easily. This stops machine parts over-heating.

LIQUID CRYSTAL

Liquid crystals have molecules that line up with each other. The result is not a solid, but something with a consistency rather like treacle. Because of the lines of molecules, light that passes through a liquid crystal may be polarized. But the effect changes depending on the temperature of the liquid crystal, and whether it carries an electric charge.

▶ If you look very closely at a calculator, you may be able to catch sight of the microcircuit which carries charges of electricity to the display panel. When a liquid crystal panel is switched on, it becomes dark so you can see it. The seven bars on a digital display are enough to make up the ten numbers from zero to nine.

vertically polarized light

crystals arranged horizontally

polarizer

front electrode

liquid crystal layer

polarizer

electric current switched on

light is absorbed

segment turns black

front polarizer

liquid crystal layer

back polarizer

reflector

electric current switched off

polarized light twisted by (90°)

light is reflected

POLARIZED LIGHT

Light rays normally vibrate in all directions. But polarized light vibrates only in one plane. If a light beam hits a liquid crystal where the molecules are arranged vertically, then only the light that vibrates vertically can pass through. A liquid crystal with molecules arranged horizontally, will then stop all of the light. The crystal looks dark. This effect appears and disappears as an electric charge is switched on and off.

LIQUID CRYSTAL DISPLAY

A liquid crystal display has two polarizing filters, with liquid crystals in between. When the current is off, the crystals turn the light through 90° so it can pass through the second filter and is reflected back. When the current is applied, the crystals line up, and the light cannot escape. This turns the segment black.

Mach

The Mach number compares the speed of a moving object (like an AIRCRAFT) in any medium (such as AIR), with the speed of sound in that medium. The speed of sound is Mach 1. Sound travels at different speeds in air, depending on height and temperature. Mach 1 is about 1200 km/h on a cold day at sea level, and 1060 km/h at the height at which an airliner flies. Subsonic travel is below the speed of sound (less than Mach 1). Travel at Mach 1 or above is SUPERSONIC.

machine

Machines are devices which change ENERGY from one form into a more useful form. Scissors are machines. They change the energy of your food, which powers your fingers, into a force that can cut paper (your fingers could never do that on their own). The earliest machine was an axe. Cranes, farming equipment and staplers are all machines. The simplest machines you normally use would include a tyre lever on your bike, and a screwdriver.

▶ A crane, axe and screwdriver are three of the six basic types of simple machine. The crane uses a pulley, the axe is a wedge and the screwdriver is an example of a screw machine.

magnesium

Magnesium is a very light silvery metal. It burns in air with a brilliant white light (it gives off a lot of ULTRAVIOLET too). Magnesium powder is used in FIREWORKS. ALLOYS of magnesium are used to make light parts for AIRCRAFT and high-performance cars.

magnet see **page 80**

magnification

Magnification is the measure of how much bigger an object is made to look by a LENS, or a curved MIRROR.

map see **page 82**

Mars

Mars is the planet nearest the EARTH. It is half as wide as the Earth, and has only one-tenth of Earth's MASS.

mass

Mass is the amount of MATTER in an object. A kilogram of LEAD has a mass of one kilogram. On the MOON it would weigh only one-sixth as much because gravity is only one-sixth as strong as it is on EARTH. But its mass would stay the same.

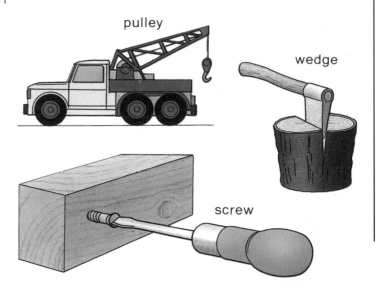

pulley

wedge

screw

MAGNETISM

In ancient times, people found rough sticks of iron ore which would attract other iron objects. When hung on a thread, these natural magnets (called lodestones) would point north/south, and were used to navigate. Iron is the only element which can be magnetized. All the atoms in the bar are lined up so that they point the same way.

▼ Both the north and south poles of a horseshoe magnet can be used to pick up an object. The invisible lines of magnetic force stretch out between the two poles.

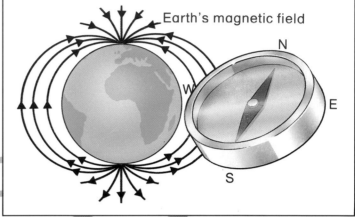

Earth's magnetic field

N

W

E

S

magnetic field of a horseshoe magnet

N

S

▲ Magnets are used as door catches. The steel magnet is fixed to the frame, and attracts a small iron bar on the edge of the door.

◄ A coil of wire around a large iron core can carry a current of electricity. When this is switched on, the iron becomes a strong electromagnet. The magnetism vanishes when the current is turned off. Electromagnets can pick up lumps of iron and steel.

N

S

▲ If you lay a piece of paper on top of a bar magnet and scatter iron filings over it, you can see the directions of the lines of force.

mathematics

Mathematics is the science of NUMBERS. Addition means putting numbers together: 4 + 5 = 9. Subtraction is done by taking one number from another: 9 − 5 = 4. In multiplication, an amount is repeated a certain number of times to give the total: 3 × 3 = 9. And division takes place when you split up a number into equal parts: 18 ÷ 2 = 9. Algebra is a form of mathematics when you use letters as symbols for unknown quantities, and GEOMETRY is the study of shapes. Trigonometry is used to work out angles and the measurement of triangles. It is important in surveying and navigation. Probability deals with chance. Suppose you have tossed a coin ten times, and it came down 'heads' each time, what is the probability it will be heads next throw? Ten to one? No! The chances are still equal. Without mathematics, many other sciences could not have developed. Physicists, engineers and computer scientists all use mathematics.

matter

Matter is the term used to describe any substance. Air is matter, so is a book. Matter is what the UNIVERSE is made of.

measurements

People have used measurements since ancient times. Many of the oldest units of measurement were based on parts of the body. A foot (about 30 centimetres) was taken from the length of a man's foot. People still talk of the height of a horse in hands (one hand equals 10 centimetres). Metric measurements were first introduced by scientists in France in the 18th century. A METRE was originally taken to be one ten-millionth of the distance from the North POLE to the equator. See **SI units**.

melting

Melting is the CHANGE OF STATE from solid to liquid. The temperature at which this occurs is the melting point. See **ice and snow, water**.

▼ These devices are used to measure different quantities. Most countries use metric measurements, but some still use the system of gallons, feet and pounds.

kitchen scales

measuring jug

stopwatch

light meter

ruler

tape measure

MAPS

A map is a drawing of an area to show features of interest. Maps usually show parts of the world, but there are brain maps or star maps, too. Road maps show you how to find your way around. Other maps allow scientists to work out the best place to drill for oil or gas. Maps are printed on paper, or produced by computer.

◀▼ This is how Europeans saw the world 2500 years ago. In the middle was the Mediterranean sea. Two thousand years later, the first maps of America were appearing. This map was published in 1545.

relief map

sea map

star map

road map

◀ Relief maps show the surface of the land. Maps of the sea-bed are important for plotting a ship's course, and in the search for minerals. Star maps help navigators, and are valuable when a new star appears. The commonest maps you see are road maps.

▶ Try making a map of your own area. You can draw the roads and mark on the school and the names of people you know. Trees and paths are important, too. In a few years, much will be altered. Your map will be an important record of how things used to be.

MAP PROJECTIONS

Maps of the world are always inaccurate! If you imagine the globe inside a grid, you can see how it becomes altered as the grid is opened out. These are the two most commonly used map projections.

Peter's projection

Mercator projection

meniscus

In a liquid, the pull between the molecules causes SURFACE TENSION. It is almost as though the liquid had a skin. If you fill a narrow tube with water the water curves at the sides of the tube. This is the meniscus.

▶ The meniscus forms at the top of a liquid. Water wets glass easily, and so its surface tends to climb up the tube a little. Mercury doesn't wet things, and keeps away from the glass by curving down.

water mercury

mercury

Mercury is the only METAL that is liquid at room temperature. It is used in THERMOMETERS because it is easy to see.

Mercury

Mercury is the name of the first PLANET of the SOLAR SYSTEM. It is not much larger than the Moon.

metals see page 84

meteor

Meteors are shooting stars. They appear as streaks of light across the night sky. They are small pieces of ROCK that hurtle through space until they hit the thick layer of AIR around the EARTH and burn up in a streak of light.

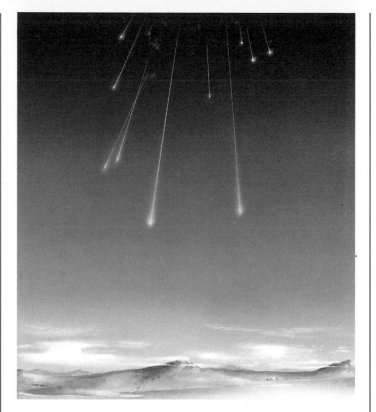

▲ Meteor showers occur when the Earth passes through a stream of dust left behind by a comet. The best showers occur around January 4, July 29, August 12, October 21 and December 14.

meteorite

Meteorites are meteors that are big enough to reach the ground without completely burning away. Usually they are the size of a brick, but some are huge enough to make large craters.

▼ A meteorite about 100 metres across and composed mostly of iron produced this crater in Arizona, USA, when it hit the Earth about 50,000 years ago.

METALS

Metals are shiny, hard elements that can be melted. They conduct heat and electricity. Metals have many important uses.

Aluminium is a soft and very light element. It has a bluish-silver colour and melts at 660°C. Among its uses are cooking foil, drink cans, and TV aerials.

Electrical wiring is usually made with **copper**. It is also used to make coins and gives fireworks a blue-green colour. Copper is often used in alloys.

Gold is a beautiful yellow metal. It is never affected by corrosion and resists acids. It is used for jewellery, electrical circuits, and to protect spacecraft.

Iron is the most widely used metal. Pure iron is soft, so it is usually made into steel. Uses include heavy pots, tools and the girders for tall buildings.

Zinc is made into many alloys. It has long been used for the cases of batteries. Steel dipped in molten zinc is said to be galvanized. It resists rusting.

Lead is a soft, heavy metal which melts at 327°C. Solder is an alloy of lead. Lead is used in roofing and to make the plates in car batteries.

Sodium is so reactive it is hardly ever used in the pure state. It can carry the heat in a nuclear reactor, and glows brilliant yellow in sodium lamps.

Calcium is very reactive. It is important for life. Calcium is found in dairy products, and also in vegetables such as spinach and rhubarb.

Titanium is very light, but not quite as light as aluminium. It does not melt until it reaches 1800°C and is very hard. It is used in steel and to make aircraft.

Tin cans are actually made of steel. They are covered with a thin layer of tin to stop them rusting. Pewter is an alloy of tin, used for decorative objects.

Mercury is the only liquid metal. It freezes solid at −39°C. Mercury is heavier than lead. It is used in barometers and also to fill thermometers.

meteorology

Meteorology is the science of studying the WEATHER. Around the POLES lie bands of cold air. Nearer the Equator the air is hotter. Temperate countries lie on the boundary between the two bands of air. Warm and cold air masses move across the land and sea. Where they meet they form areas of low pressure called CYCLONES, and belts of rain, called fronts.

▼ The main factors that affect the weather are air pressure, air temperature, and the speed and direction of the wind. Meteorologists record these conditions to prepare a weather forecast.

methane

Methane is a flammable gas containing hydrogen and carbon. Its formula is CH_4. Methane forms from decaying organic MATTER underground and is found in natural gas. See **recycling**.

metre

Originally, a metre was a unit taken from MEASURING the EARTH. It is now set at a more scientific value. A metre (1m) is defined as the distance that light travels in a vacuum in 1/299792458th of a second.

metric system

Metric MEASUREMENT is built on seven base units. The metre is the base unit for length, the kilogram for mass. Each unit is divided (or multiplied) into further points which are ten times smaller or larger. The prefix of each unit tells you how it relates to base unit. For example, a *centi*metre means one hundredth of a metre. A *milli*metre is a thousandth of a metre. The metric system is the system of measuring around the scientific world. The old system of using pounds, feet and gallons has been replaced in many countries.

microchip

A microchip is the complex system of LEADS, TRANSISTORS and other components which is made on a single wafer of SILICON. This INTEGRATED CIRCUIT is then mounted in a plastic block. Microchips are used in COMPUTERS.

micrometer

A micrometer is a screw gauge used by engineers for measuring the diameter or thickness of small objects very accurately.

▼ The thickness of a small object may be measured by clamping it in the jaws of a micrometer. Its thickness is then read off a scale on the side of the instrument.

micrometre

Microscopic objects are measured in micrometres, or millionths of a metre.

M

microphone

A microphone converts sound waves into ELECTRICAL signals. Inside a microphone is a diaphragm, a thin sheet of paper or plastic, which is vibrated by sounds. The diaphragm is connected to a MAGNET. When the diaphragm vibrates, the magnet's movements produce electricity in a nearby coil. The pattern of electrical signals represents the original sounds. A LOUDSPEAKER can convert these electrical signals back to SOUND.

microprocessor

A microprocessor is an INTEGRATED CIRCUIT or MICROCHIP which processes data in a COMPUTER. The central processing units in early computers had transistors and other components soldered together and they were very large. Now they are made by projecting a reduced image of a template onto a tiny light-sensitive silicon chip. The entire central processing unit can fit onto a chip the size of your fingernail. The chip is held in a plastic mount.

microscope

How do you look at something very small? You bring it closer to your eye. The trouble is that if you bring the object too close your eye can no longer focus on it. A microscope allows you to study tiny objects that your eye cannot make out. The LENS is the important part of a microscope. It bends LIGHT shining through the object before it reaches your eye, so the object appears larger than it really is. The simple microscope has just one lens which MAGNIFIES specimens. But even a simple microscope allows you to see bacteria. Compound microscopes have several lenses, to make the picture

▲ A thin, transparent specimen placed on the specimen table of a light microscope is magnified by the objective lens and viewed through the eyepiece lens. A selection of objective lenses give different magnifications.

even sharper. Simple microscopes can magnify up to 500 times; compound microscopes about 2000 times. An ELECTRON MICROSCOPE uses a beam of electrons to magnify dry objects in a VACUUM. Electron microscopes can magnify hundreds of thousands of times. Scanning electron microscopes show surface features, and a tunnelling microscope can reveal details of the position of atoms. Other microscopes use x-rays and ultraviolet rays.

MICROWAVES

Microwaves are a form of radiation with a wavelength that is between radio waves and infrared waves. Like radio waves, they can travel long distances. But, like infrared, they can produce heat. They are reflected by metal surfaces, but cannot penetrate deeply through softer substances. When they do penetrate, they release heat energy, as in microwave ovens.

▼ Microwaves are produced be a special generator known as a magnetron. The invention of small magnetrons made the microwave oven possible.

▼ A rotating microwave reflector, and a turntable plate help spread the radiation so the food is cooked evenly.

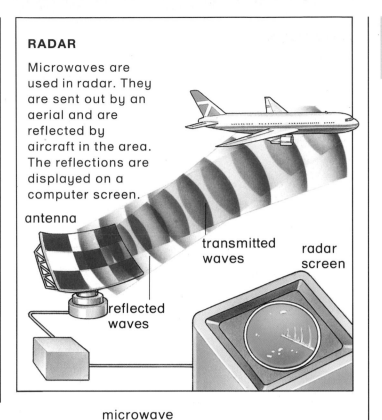

RADAR

Microwaves are used in radar. They are sent out by an aerial and are reflected by aircraft in the area. The reflections are displayed on a computer screen.

antenna

transmitted waves

radar screen

reflected waves

fan

microwave beam

magnetron

controls

reflected waves

turntable

▲ The microwave radiation agitates the molecules of water within food and it heats up rapidly. Food is heated from the inside.

▲ The door catch controls the magnetron. When the door is opened, the microwave switches off. The controls on the front panel allow you to set the strength of radiation, and the time.

M

Milky Way

The EARTH and the rest of the SOLAR SYSTEM are part of a GALAXY which is called the Milky Way. If you look out to space at night through the thin part of the galaxy, you see the darkness of space beyond our galaxy most clearly. But if you turn to look through the thickness of the galaxy, you see millions of other stars. They are our neighbours in the galaxy. There are so many that they make the whole sky look 'milky'. The Milky Way is a spiral galaxy which is 100,000 LIGHT YEARS across and 1000 light years thick. It contains about 100 billion stars. The Solar System is near the edge of the galaxy, which is why we get such a good view of the rest of space.

▲ Every star visible in the night sky belongs to the Milky Way galaxy.

minerals

Minerals are natural ELEMENTS or COMPOUNDS which make up ROCKS. They often form beautiful CRYSTALS. GEMS, METAL ORES, SAND, SALTS and even talc are all kinds of minerals.

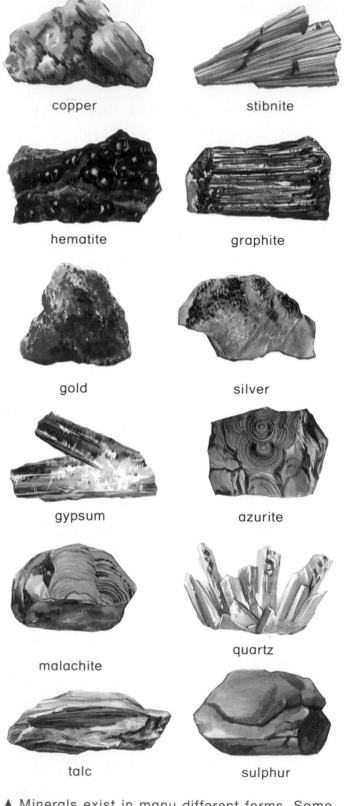

copper

stibnite

hematite

graphite

gold

silver

gypsum

azurite

malachite

quartz

talc

sulphur

▲ Minerals exist in many different forms. Some are glassy crystals, others are like brightly coloured rocks. Minerals may be elements, such as gold or sulphur, or compounds such as metal ores. Many minerals are used for jewellery.

mirage

A mirage sometimes appears when layers of AIR near the ground become hot. The hot air can act as a LENS, bending rays of light. Instead of the ground you may see an image of the sky reflected by the hot air. It looks as if there is water ahead. This is called a mirage. You can see this effect on a hot road in summer.

mirror

Smooth and polished surfaces reflect light. These act as mirrors. A flat mirror shows you back to front – your left side appears to be your right in the mirror image. A curved mirror can act like a LENS by bending light rays to form a magnified image. Wavy mirrors in fairgrounds make you look really weird.

▶ The shape of a mirror affects the image it produces. A flat mirror reflects light at the same angle at which it hits the mirror, producing an undistorted image.

reflected light

flat mirror

▶ Concave mirrors reflect light inwards and magnify the image.

concave mirror

▶ Convex mirrors reflect light outwards and produce a smaller image.

convex mirror

missile

A missile is something that is thrown. A spear is a missile, so is a stone that breaks a window. Weapons which are sent up by rocket and guided to their targets are missiles too.

modem

Digital information in BINARY form can be changed to an ANALOGUE sound signal and sent down a telephone wire to a COMPUTER or FAX machine. The device that changes the signal is a modem. The name comes from the words MOdulator and DEModulator.

molecule

A molecule is the smallest particle of a COMPOUND or ELEMENT that can exist on its own. It is a group of atoms joined together by forces called bonds.

▲ If a car stops suddenly, the momentum of the driver and passengers keeps them moving. They are stopped by applying a force in the opposite direction. This is provided by a seat belt.

momentum

A moving body tends to keep moving unless an outside force stops it. This is the principle of INERTIA. The amount of ENERGY the body has depends on its MASS and its VELOCITY. Momentum is measured by multiplying mass by velocity. If a car stops suddenly, the passengers' momentum carries them on until they hit the inside of the car, unless they are stopped by a seatbelt or an air-bag.

M

monorail

A train which runs on a single rail is a monorail (*mono* is Greek for 'one'). Some monorail trains are raised on magnets and are pushed along by powerful linear motors. This is known as magnetic levitation (maglev for short).

electromagnets

▲ Opposite poles of a magnet push each other away, or repel. This force is used to support a Maglev train. Electromagnets on the track and the underside of the train repel each other, lifting the train off the track.

like poles repel

unlike poles attract

monsoon

The monsoon season is caused when bands of hot and cold AIR meet in the tropics. A monsoon is a tropical wind that occurs at a particular time of year and blows constantly in one direction. It brings heavy rains. See **meteorology**.

▲ The heavily cratered Moon always shows the same face as it orbits the Earth.

moon

The Moon is our nearest neighbour in space, about 382,000 kilometres from Earth. The Moon is about 4500 million years old, and it is 3476 kilometres in diameter. Its mass is only about one-hundredth of the Earth's mass. The Moon orbits the Earth once every 27.32 days, but (because the Earth is moving round at the same time) the time from one New Moon to the next is 29.53 days.

▼ Sunshine lights up half of the Moon, but we cannot always see all of the lit half from Earth. The result is that the Moon goes through a 29-day cycle, the phases of the Moon.

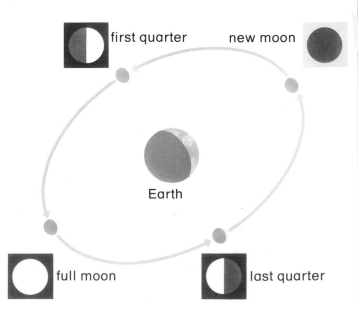

first quarter

new moon

Earth

full moon

last quarter

motor

A motor is a device which turns energy into movement. An ELECTRIC current passing through a coil in a MAGNETIC field will make the coil move. This is the idea behind an electric motor. An INTERNAL COMBUSTION engine is a motor in which FUEL is burned to produce power.

▼ In this simple electric motor, a battery supplies electric current to a wire coil in a magnetic field. This makes the coil rotate.

battery
permanent magnet
North pole
carbon brushes
rotating wire loop
South pole

mountain

Mountains are high hills with steep slopes. Most mountain ranges are found where huge land masses have crashed into each other pushing the layers of rock

DID YOU KNOW?

Millions of years ago, as the continents drifted towards their present positions, India crashed into Asia. As a result of this great collision the Himalayan mountains were formed. The rocks between the two land masses were forced upwards, and the ancient sea bed ended up at the top of the Himalayas.

Asia
India

Himalayas
India

upwards over millions of years. Others are formed by faults and folding of the rocks in the Earth's crust. The highest mountain ranges are also the youngest. The oldest mountains, such as in Scotland, have been gradually worn down by the forces of EROSION. See **plate tectonics**.

▼ When plates of land push against one another, some of the rocks may be thrust upwards to form mountains. The land may fold or it may break and push up large blocks of rock.

fold mountains
pressure

block mountains
pressure

movement

Movement is a change of position in an object, like the movement of the hand of a clock. Motion is when an object goes to a different place, like a car along a road (in which the pistons are in movement).

▼ Because a snake has no legs it moves either by pushing out sideways and to the rear, in a zig-zag movement, or by sending a rippling (concertina) movement straight along its body.

zigzag movement

pushing action
concertina movement
grips

N

natural gas see **methane**

nebula

The word nebula was first used by ancient astronomers to describe a luminous spot in the sky. TELESCOPES showed there are also many dark nebulae. Nebulae are great clouds of fine dust and gas that give rise to new STARS or are thrown out when a star dies. Many nebulae are bigger than GALAXIES.

▼ Newborn stars shine brightly in the centre of the Orion nebula. A dark horsehead-shaped cloud stands out against the bright gas behind.

neon

Neon is one of the 'inert gases'. This means that it hardly ever forms COMPOUNDS, because its atoms will not react with other atoms. But neon still has a use. If you put a strong charge of ELECTRICITY across a tube containing some neon, then the neon glows bright red. Neon lights are used to make colourful advertising signs. See **lighting**.

Neptune

Neptune is the eighth of the nine known planets of the SOLAR SYSTEM. It is 50,000 kilometres across, and it takes 164.82 Earth years to orbit the SUN. The Voyager space probe passed Neptune in 1989 and revealed that it has faint rings and at least eight moons. The surface temperature of Neptune is −210°C, with winds of up to 2000km/h whipping across it.

neutron

A neutron is one of the particles in the nucleus of an ATOM. It is similar to a PROTON, but it has no electric charge. When an atom is broken apart (in a nuclear reaction), neutrons may be shot out. Each one can then make nearby atoms split, starting a chain reaction. A neutron bomb is an atomic weapon which gives out large amounts of neutrons. It kills people, but does not damage buildings.

neutron star

Neutron stars are the smallest and heaviest STARS. They are formed when a SUPERNOVA collapses. Geninga is a neutron star only 20–30 kilometres in diameter, yet it is heavier than the Sun. Some neutron stars flash and are called PULSARS.

Newton

Sir Isaac Newton (1643 – 1727) was the philosopher who worked out the laws of GRAVITY. He also studied LIGHT rays and MATHEMATICS. When there was an outbreak of Black Death (the plague) in 1665 he left Cambridge University and went to stay with his parents in the Lincolnshire village where he was born. This gave him time to work out some of his best ideas. He returned to Cambridge in 1667.

nickel

Nickel is a silvery METAL which does not easily CORRODE or go dull. It is often used to make electrical connections in computers and instruments in operating theatres. It is commonly made into coins, too (which is why the 'nickel' is a five-cent American coin).

nicotine

Nicotiana is the tobacco plant, and nicotine is a poisonous chemical found in the leaves, which are used to make cigars and cigarettes. Nicotine has also been used as an insect spray by gardeners.

nitrates

Nitrates are COMPOUNDS of nitric ACID. Nitrates all contain NITROGEN. Some explode violently, and are used to make weapons. Other nitrates are used to make fertilizers for the soil, because all living things need nitrogen to grow. If too much fertilizer is used, it can be washed into waterways. The nitrates fertilize waterweed in the rivers and canals, and they become clogged.

nitrogen

Nitrogen forms 80 percent of the atmosphere. Its CHEMICAL symbol is N. Nitrogen COMPOUNDS are vital to all living things. They are needed for growth.

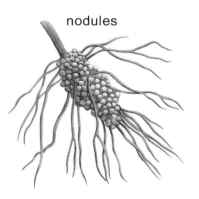

nodules

◄ Plants need nitrogen, but they cannot absorb it from the air. Some plants have nodules on their roots containing bacteria that change the gas into compounds called nitrates which plants can absorb.

nitroglycerine

Nitroglycerine is an oily liquid which burns if it is spilled, but explodes violently if it is suddenly struck or heated. To use it safely it is soaked into sawdust or clay to make dynamite. Dynamite was invented by a Swedish industrialist, Alfred Nobel. He gave the profits from his invention to set up the Nobel Prizes.

noise

Noise is the kind of SOUND that annoys people. Electrical noise is the 'hiss' behind a signal in systems like TELEVISION.

nova

A nova is a new STAR, caused by a gigantic explosion in space.

numbers see **page 95**

nylon

Nylon is a PLASTIC made up of very long thin MOLECULES. Nylon fibres are used to make clothes, and bristles for toothbrushes. Nylon is also made into parts for machines and artificial hip-joints.

NUCLEAR POWER

The nucleus of an atom can be broken apart to produce energy. Einstein's theory of relativity showed that a small mass can be changed into a huge amount of energy. In a nuclear reactor, neutrons are fired into the nuclei at very high speed. As the nuclei are hit, they break apart and shoot out still more neutrons. This can start a chain reaction, producing vast amounts of energy.

▼ The breaking of atoms to release energy is called nuclear fission. The fuel used in nuclear reactors is an isotope of uranium. Some nations make most of their electricity this way.

▼ Radioactive waste is the problem with nuclear power. But coal power stations release waste gases. Both damage the environment.

neutron

uranium atom

A NUCLEAR POWER STATION

reactor   condenser   steam   cooling tower

exhaust steam out   water

steam in   turbine   generator   transformer

Nuclear power stations do not make electricity out of radioactivity. They use the heat energy released during nuclear fission to produce steam. The pressure of the steam drives an electric generator. Nuclear power produces no greenhouse gases, but people are worried about the risk of accidents.

▼ The nuclear reaction is controlled by sliding graphite rods in and out of the reactor core. Graphite absorbs neutrons, so the chain reaction is slowed.

control rods   heat exchanger   steam out   coolant out   coolant in   pump   water in   reactor core

NUMBERS

Numbers can be read in any language. You would not find it easy to read a text in a different language, but numbers are a universal language. The system we use now is based on 'Arabic numerals', but many other systems have been used in the past. The Romans used a series of lines – I, II, III, IV, V and so on – because they were easier to carve on stone.

NUMBER GAMES

The number 142,857 has almost magical properties. It is a 'circular number'. Multiply it by numbers up to 7: 1 x 142,857 = 142,857; 2 x 142,857 = 285,714; 3 x 142,857 = 428,571; 4 x 142,857 = 571,428; 5 x 142,857 = 714,285; 6 x 142,857 = 857,142. Each answer is the same series of numbers (starting at a different place each time). For higher numbers it doesn't work: 7 x 142,857 = 999,999. But divide 1 by 7 on your calculator and see what number you get!

Try this one. Ask a friend to write their age three times; 13 become 131313. Study it for a moment and then predict that it can be divided by seven. This works for all numbers between 10 and 99.

◄ Numbers increase hugely if you keep doubling them up. The series goes: 1, 2, 4, 8, 16, 32, 64, 128 and so on. This is a geometrical progression. Adding the same number at each stages gives a far lower rate of increase. This is known as an arithmetical progression.

► Calculators are invaluable for performing calculations with large numbers. They use microchips to carry out difficult operations in a fraction of a second.

Roman

I	II	III	IV	V	VI	VII	VIII	IX	X
1	2	3	4	5	6	7	8	9	10

Mayan

| 1 | 2 | 3 | 4 | 5 | 6 | 7 |
| 8 | 9 | 10 |

Chinese

一	二	三	四	五	六	七
1	2	3	4	5	6	7

八	九	十	十五	五十
8	9	10	15	50

Hindi

१	२	३	४	५	६	७	८	९	१०
1	2	3	4	5	6	7	8	9	10

▲ Most ancient number systems did not use the number zero. Zero was invented by Hindu mathematicians in about AD600.

▼ The numbers on a watch are usually Arabic, but some have Roman numerals. The numbers on a digital watchface are made up from seven segments.

Arabic numbers

Roman numbers

digital display

O

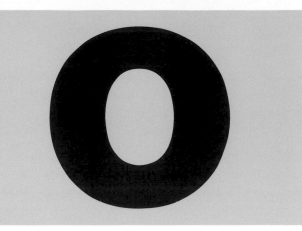

ocean

The oceans cover over two-thirds of the Earth. The largest, and also the oldest, is the Pacific Ocean. The average depth of the oceans is about four kilometres, and their average temperature is 4°C. The five oceans are: the Atlantic, the Pacific, the Indian, the Arctic and the Antarctic.

octane

Octane is a liquid PETROCHEMICAL produced from crude OIL. Octane burns easily. Samples of other types of fuel are compared with octane to see how well they burn in an engine.

▼ The octane molecule is so-called because it is made from eight carbon atoms which are linked to 18 hydrogen atoms. Materials made from hydrogen and carbon are called hydrocarbons.

● carbon
○ hydrogen

▼ Two thirds of the Earth's surface is covered by five major oceans. Water constantly evaporates from the oceans into the atmosphere and eventually falls back to Earth as rain.

Northwest Passage
Arctic Ocean
East Siberian Sea
Baffin Bay
Chukchi Sea
Beaufort Sea
3
5
6
1
4
Sea of Okhotsk
Hudson Bay
North Sea
7
Baltic Sea
Gulf of Alaska
2
Black Sea
Gulf of Mexico
North Atlantic Ocean
Persian Gulf
South China Sea
Sea of Japan
North Pacific Ocean
Caribbean Sea
Mediterranean Sea
8
Red Sea
Bismark Sea
South Atlantic Ocean
Arabian Sea
Coral Sea
Indian Ocean
South Pacific Ocean
Great Australian Bight
Tasman Sea

1 David Straight
2 Labrador Sea
3 Greenland Sea
4 Norwegian Sea
5 Barents Sea
6 Lapteu Sea
7 Bering Sea
8 Philippine Sea

Antarctic Ocean

conveyor belt

powerful light source

light rays

lens

powerful light source

◄ Machines using optical character recognition systems can sort letters automatically by reading the post codes printed on the envelopes.

oil

An oil is a slippery liquid which does not mix with water. Oils are often produced by living cells as an energy store. Oil from fossil plants can be collected by drilling oil-wells. This is crude oil. Crude oil contains hydrocarbons – compounds made up of only hydrogen and carbon. Because oils are rich in energy they make good FUELS. And because they are slippery they are used as LUBRICANTS.

▲ Oil and natural gas are found far underground. To reach the oil, a well is drilled down through the layers of rock from an oil rig. Pipelines carry the crude oil to a refinery where it is treated.

optical character recognition

This is a system that allows COMPUTERS to read printed type. A scanner recognizes the shape of the characters and sends the information to the computer. A special kind of type has been developed that is easier for computers to read. The letters are made up of thick and thin lines, so they are easy to recognize.

optical fibre

An optical fibre is a hair-like thread of glass. Light shone into an optical fibre is reflected back from the surface of the glass, and so it cannot escape. If the glass is of high quality (and very clear) the light travels for great distances. Pulses of light from a laser can be used to carry DIGITAL information. This is faster than sending electricty along a wire. In hospitals, optical fibre systems are used to look inside patients' bodies.

▼ Optical fibres carry information in the form of light beams bouncing between the glass walls.

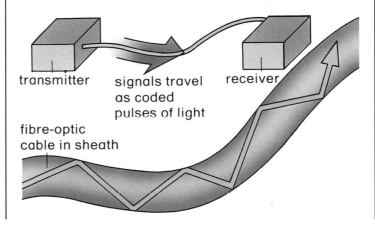

transmitter

signals travel as coded pulses of light

receiver

fibre-optic cable in sheath

O

optical illusions

The eye picks out certain items of information in a picture, and your brain uses this to work out what you are looking at. If you send information to the eye which it does not expect, you can play tricks with your sight. Circles can become ovals, and straight lines can look curved.

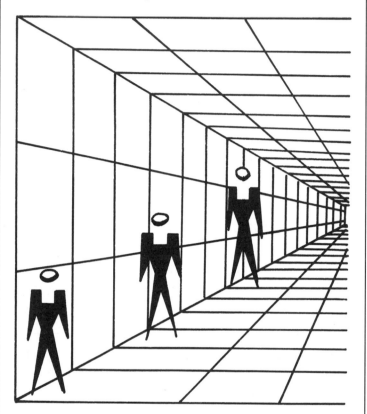

▲ ▼ The figure on the right appears taller than the others, but they are all the same height. The vertical lines appear to bend, but they are straight. The backgrounds trick the brain.

▲ Although we often talk about planets 'circling' the Sun, the orbits of the planets are actually slightly squashed circles called ellipses.

orbit

Bodies that move around each other in space are in orbit. The MOON orbits the EARTH in this way. GRAVITY keeps pulling the Moon and Earth together, but their MOTION keeps them apart. See **Solar System**, **spacecraft**.

ore

Ores are MINERALS which are rich in COMPOUNDS of METALS. They can be crushed up and treated in order to extract the metal. Some ores (like malachite, an ore of COPPER) are beautifully coloured.

oxide

Oxides are COMPOUNDS formed when an ELEMENT reacts with OXYGEN. Rust is iron oxide; water is HYDROGEN oxide.

oxygen

Oxygen is the second most common ELEMENT in AIR. Its chemical symbol is O. Oxygen will combine actively with many other elements. Large amounts of ENERGY may be released when this occurs. Many substances burn when they react with oxygen, like the COMBUSTION of wood in a fire. CHEMICALS inside your body react with oxygen too, which is where your energy comes from.

ozone

ATOMS of OXYGEN usually join together in pairs, and oxygen gas has the formula O_2. With extra ENERGY they can join in threes, and this is the gas known as ozone (O_3). It is responsible for the 'electrical smell' of electronic apparatus. Ozone is poisonous. The ozone layer forms in the stratosphere, 30 kilometres above the Earth. The ozone molecules filter out the dangerous ULTRAVIOLET rays from the SUN, and protect us from their effects. Some AEROSOLS contain CHLOROFLUOROCARBONS (CFCs), which are thought to damage the ozone layer. The use of CFCs is strictly controlled in many countries.

▼ The ozone layer, at a height of 30 kilometres in the atmosphere, protects us from the harmful effects of ultraviolet radiation from the Sun.

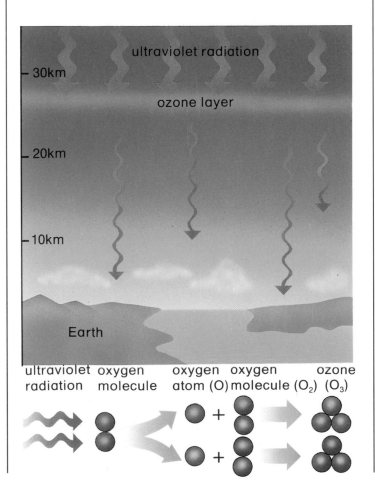

ultraviolet radiation

30km

ozone layer

20km

10km

Earth

| ultraviolet radiation | oxygen molecule | oxygen atom (O) | oxygen molecule (O_2) | ozone (O_3) |

palaeontology

Palaeontology is the science of FOSSILS. When living things die they are sometimes buried in a layer of mud. After millions of years the mud turns to solid ROCK and the remains are preserved as fossils. Each layer of rock can be dated and this tells us the age of the fossils. By studying the fossils, palaeontologists have discovered much about life forms that died out millions of years ago. Most exciting are the fossils of dinosaurs, some of which were as large as a house. Palaeontologists know not only what the dinosaurs looked like, but also how they lived and what they ate.

▼ When palaeontologists find fossils, they carefully dig up the remains and take them to a laboratory to be cleaned and identified.

▶ Paper is made mostly from trees. Logs are ground into wood pulp, and mixed with water. The mixture passes onto a wire mesh which traps the wood fibres and forms a web of paper. The paper is then rolled and dried.

paper

In ancient times, people used to write on animal skin or thin sheets of plant material, like papyrus. But about two thousand years ago the Chinese found out how to make a thin paste of vegetable fibres, and let it dry out in a sheet. This was how paper was first made. Most paper is made from wood, but RECYCLED paper is made from paper waste.

parachute

A parachute is a large 'umbrella' of light cloth. Its large area creates high AIR resistance so people can float safely down to the ground. Parachutes are also used to slow down racing-cars or planes at the end of their run.

parsec

A parsec is a measurement used in ASTRONOMY. It is the distance you would have to travel so that the Sun and Earth looked as if they were only one degree second (1/3600th of a degree) apart in space. A parsec equals 3.26 light years, or 30,857,000,000,000 kilometres.

particle

Particles are tiny objects. Some particles are visible, such as sand-grains. Others, such as PROTONS, are tinier than an ATOM.

pendulum

Any object which swings freely back and forth at the end of a rod or string is a pendulum. The number of swings it makes each minute depends only on the length of the pendulum, and not (as you might think) on the weight of the object at the end. See **Foucault**.

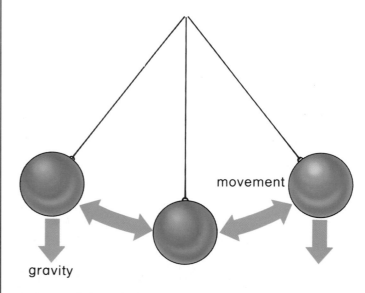

▲ A pendulum is a weight on the end of a string. When the weight, called a bob, swings out to one side, gravity pulls it back. If left to swing, air resistance eventually slows it down to a halt.

periscope

A periscope is a tube with a peep-hole at one end and an angled mirror at each end. It allows you to see higher (or lower) than normal, or around a corner. The mirrors reflect light from the object

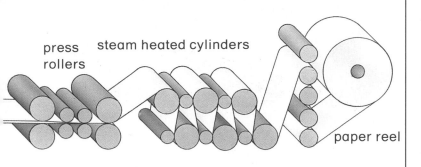

press rollers   steam heated cylinders

paper reel

▲ In this perpetual motion machine the ballbearings were supposed to turn the wheel, which would drive the screw round and lift the balls back to the top. However, energy is lost as friction, so the machine could never work.

towards your eyes, so you can see around obstacles. Periscopes are used in submarines to look above the surface of the sea. Scientists have used them to look inside nuclear reactors.

perpetual motion

For many years inventors tried to make a machine which would work without using energy. It would then keep turning forever, by perpetual motion. But nothing can work without using some energy, so perpetual motion is impossible. Many different designs were tried out, but all of them were bound to fail.

petrochemicals

Petrochemicals are chemicals made from crude OIL (petroleum) and NATURAL GAS. They include fuel for cars and trucks, and are used to make PLASTICS and synthetic rubber, DRUGS and many other CHEMICALS.

▼ A wide range of household products, plastics, artificial rubber, soap, cosmetics, and animal food are made from petrochemicals.

synthetic rubber

polyurethane

melamine

animal feed

polyester

vinyl

nylon

polythene

cosmetics

nylon

nylon

soap

vinyl

synthetic rubber

household cleaners

polystyrene

charged
image area

finished copies

mirrors

page being
copied

lens

toner dust

drum

heater

copy being made

plain
copying
paper

pharmacology
Pharmacology is the study of DRUGS and how they work. Another science, pharmacognosy, deals with how drugs are discovered.

phosphorus
We all contain small amounts of phosphorus. It is found in bones, blood and teeth. Pure phosphorus is a very active ELEMENT. It burns easily, and is used to make match-heads. The symbol for phosphorus is P.

▶ Matches burn when they are 'struck' because the match-head or the strip on the box contains phosphorus.

photocopier
It is hard to imagine modern life without photocopiers. A photocopier produces an exact copy of the image on a page. At one time, the best way to copy a document

▲ A photocopier works by making a powdered pigment called toner stick to a blank sheet of paper in a pattern that exactly matches the ink on the original page.

was to type it all out by hand. An American lawyer, Chester Carlson, became so tired of this work he decided to find a better way. This is how the idea of photocopying was born. When you photocopy something an image of the page is projected onto a drum, and a static electric charge is transferred to the drum wherever the image is dark (where there is text or pictures). The electric charge attracts toner dust onto the drum and it is then transferred to a blank sheet of paper. A heater fixes the toner to the paper and the result is a perfect copy of the original. The first photocopier went on sale in 1950.

photography see **page 103**

photon
The photon is a unit of LIGHT ENERGY. It has no mass when it is at rest, but scientists can measure its momentum when it is travelling at the speed of light.

PHOTOGRAPHY

Photography means 'drawing a picture with light'. The scene is focused onto film by a lens. Behind the lens a shutter keeps out the light, except for the moment when the button is pressed. Then it opens for a split second to allow a certain amount of light onto the film. The light affects the chemicals in the film and produces a permanent image.

▶ Colour film is made up of six layers. Separate layers absorb blue, green and red light. In this way the whole picture is recorded. A plastic base supports the film, and a dark backing absorbs any remaining light.

light

◀ The size of the shutter hole is the aperture. The length of time the shutter is open is called the exposure time. Automatic cameras have a small light sensor. This sets the exposure for a longer time if the light is dull. When the picture has been taken, the film winds on, ready for the next shot.

flash

viewfinder

lens

film

film

shutter (open)

aperture

light from object

DID YOU KNOW?

Holiday snaps often show the people too far away. All you see is a few stone columns and some tiny figures. This does not make an interesting photograph.

Remember to keep the buildings at a distance. This way you can get most of them into the picture. But do the opposite with the people: keep them near the camera (about three metres). You can still see the building in the background. But take care not to slant the camera, or the Leaning Tower of Pisa may end up looking perfectly upright.

103

P

physics

Physics is the science of studying matter and energy. This includes LIGHT, SOUND, ELECTRICITY, MAGNETS, RADIATION and moving objects. Nuclear physics studies the particles inside the atom and the energy they contain. This lead to the development of nuclear energy. Many physicists are trying to find energy sources which do not cause pollution.

piezoelectricity

Some crystals (such as QUARTZ) will change mechanical energy into electricity if you squeeze them. Gas lighters often work like this, creating a spark when you squeeze a trigger. It works the other way round, too. An electrical charge on a piezoelectric crystal produces movement. This is how a quartz watch works.

▼ Some gas heaters have a piezoelectric igniter. Pushing the button bends a piezoelectric crystal and creates a spark, which lights the gas.

gas heater

ignition button

piezoelectric unit

current produced

spark lights gas

gas pipe

planet

A planet is a body which orbits a star. Stars, like our Sun, are hot and give out light, which illuminates the planets. There are nine known planets in our Solar System. Some, like the Earth, are made of rock and metal, but the huge planets like Jupiter are mostly gas.

▲ The planets grew out of the spinning ring of gas and dust left over from the formation of the Sun. Solid particles stuck together forming larger bodies which eventually became the planets. The Sun's gravity holds them in orbit.

PLASTICS

Plastic are made by joining molecules together in chains. Plastics are polymers ('poly' means lots, and 'merus' means parts). They are synthetic. In nature, things like cotton and fingernails are the closest to man-made plastics. There are lots of kinds of plastic, such as PVC, perspex and polythene, all with different properties. Look around and you will see how much plastic there is.

DID YOU KNOW?

Many plastics, such as polythene and polystyrene melt when they are heated. They can then be moulded into shape and are used to make household objects. If they become hot, they will melt again. These are thermoplastics.

polystyrene

bakelite

A second group of plastics set hard when heated. These are thermosetting plastics. Bakelite is one example, and so is glue made from plastic resin.

glue

polythene

▼ Molecules of ethene, a gas, contain two carbon atoms and four of hydrogen. There are two bonds between the carbons.

▼ As only one bond is needed to hold the carbon atoms together, the ethene molecules can be joined together. This forms polythene.

double bond

ethene

carbon

hydrogen

single bond

▶▼ Plastics are not normally biodegradable. There are no microbes that can use them as food when they are dumped as waste. This can be useful – you don't want biodegradable plastic water pipes. But the plastic packaging on many objects causes pollution.

PLATE TECTONICS

Have you ever noticed how the coastlines of America and Africa fit together? It looks as if they have been torn apart. Alfred Wegener, a German geologist, noticed this, and published a theory in 1915 that the continents were drifting. Plate tectonics explains how they move. The Earth's crust is made up of huge plates of rock. The movements of these plates causes the continents to drift around the Earth's surface.

▶ The present-day continents are the parts of huge plates of the Earth's crust which are higher than the sea. They are all moving very slowly. South Africa and America are drifting apart. They are moving at the same speed as your finger-nails grow.

today

direction of drift

future

▲ Hundreds of millions of years in the future, North and South America may have split apart. Australia may collide with Asia.

▼ Three hundred million years ago there was a single mass of land. It is given the name Pangaea. As time went by, this 'super-continent' broke up.

▼ One large mass of land drifted off to eventually become Asia whilst North and South America, drifted off to the west. Africa can be seen near the middle.

Pangaea

300 million years ago

▼ Where the plates meet, the ocean floor sinks down towards deeper layers of the Earth. This area is the 'subduction zone'. Volcanoes are common near the edges of plates like these.

continental plates

volcano

subduction zone

sea floor

crust

crust

movement of plate

plate sinks

mantle

hot molten rock

platinum

Platinum is a precious METAL that never corrodes or becomes dull. It is a silvery colour and is sometimes used to make electrical contacts. It is used as a CATALYST in CATALYTIC CONVERTERS.

Pluto

Pluto is the outermost of the SUN'S PLANETS. It is smaller than the MOON, and it takes 248.6 Earth years to orbit the Sun. See **Solar System**.

plutonium

Plutonium is used to make ATOMIC bombs. Its symbol is Pu. Plutonium has 238 PARTICLES in the nucleus of each atom. But if an extra NEUTRON is injected in a nuclear reactor it forms plutonium-239. This breaks down easily, releasing a lot of ENERGY, and can cause an EXPLOSION.

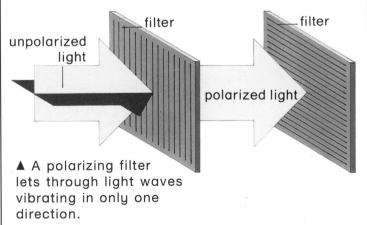

▲ A polarizing filter lets through light waves vibrating in only one direction.

polarized light

A beam of LIGHT contains different wavelengths which vibrate at every angle. Polarized light has waves which all vibrate in only one direction. A polarizing filter polarizes light by allowing through only the light which vibrates in one direction. A second filter at right angles would stop all the light.

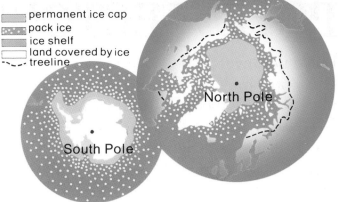

permanent ice cap
pack ice
ice shelf
land covered by ice
treeline

North Pole

South Pole

▲ The South Pole is mainly land covered by ice. The North Pole is ice floating on an ocean.

Poles

If you think of the EARTH turning on a pole, you can see how the North and South geographic Poles obtained their names. The Earth also has magnetic poles, just like a giant magnet. They are 11.5° away from the geographic poles. See **compass**.

pollution see **pages 108 and 109**

polygon

A polygon is a shape with many straight edges. They are often named after the number of sides they have. *Hexa* means six in Greek, *tri* means three.

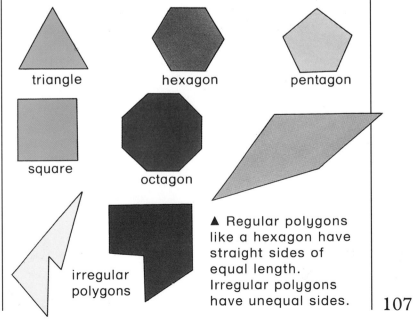

triangle   hexagon   pentagon

square   octagon

irregular polygons

▲ Regular polygons like a hexagon have straight sides of equal length. Irregular polygons have unequal sides.

POLLUTION

Pollution is caused by people. It occurs when when we overload the Earth with waste. Pollution has many sources. Factories, power stations, cars and agriculture all produce harmful waste chemicals. The waste is released into the air and into the rivers and oceans. Some is buried on land. Pollution affects the air we breathe, it kills wildlife and destroys the environment.

Many people want the latest product. It may be new shoes or the latest car. Factories work day and night to make these goods. They use energy and pollute the air with waste gases that can be dangerous.

Every litre of fuel burned by a car or a plane gives out more than 60 litres of greenhouse gases. Too many cars add to global warming.

Noise pollution is a big problem in many cities. Airports, industries and traffic can cause a deafening noise. Quarries, rubbish dumps and power plants spoil the landscape. This is called visual pollution.

air pollution

nuclear pollution

radioactive waste

noise pollution

freshwater pollution

slag heaps

landfill sites

visual pollution

opencast mining

sewage

▶ Oil tankers are sometimes wrecked and huge oil slicks are formed. They destroy beaches and kill thousands of birds and other sea animals.

oil slick

Rivers are polluted by sewage, pesticides and fertilizers from agriculture, and toxic waste from factories. Some of these chemicals may be dumped against the law. They harm the river's wildlife.

The huge amount of waste we produce is often buried in landfill sites. Many old sites are leaking, and water supplies may be contaminated with poisonous chemicals. Landfills also produce methane gas.

Air pollution comes from many sources. Burning coal and oil releases toxic compounds as well as carbon dioxide. CFCs from aerosols and packaging foam harm the ozone layer which protects life from ultraviolet radiation.

Pollution from industrial centres is found across the open countryside as well as in the seas. The poisonous elements that get into the environment include zinc, lead, arsenic, mercury and cadmium. Waste contains materials that could be recycled instead of being thrown away.

greenhouse gases

acid rain

smog

steam and water vapour from cooling towers

◄ Much of our waste eventually ends up in the sea. Surveys have shown that seals, whales and polar bears have pesticides in their bodies. Our pollution can spread thousands of kilometres across the Earth.

marine pollution

thermal pollution

waste dumped at sea

industrial waste

pesticides

fertilizers

exhaust fumes

109

P

polymer

Polymers are formed by joining together lots of identical MOLECULES. Ethene is a sweet-smelling gas. Join millions of ethene molecules together and you have polythene (polyethene), a PLASTIC.

positron

A positron is a tiny PARTICLE like an ELECTRON, but with a positive charge. Positrons are a kind of antimatter because they are the opposite of normal matter.

▲ Potassium reacts violently with water. If a piece of potassium is dropped into water, it skates around the surface spitting flames.

potassium

Potassium is a light, soft metal. Its symbol is K (because the Latin for potassium is *kalium*). Potassium is such an active ELEMENT that it burns if you let air get at it. It is kept under OIL in a jar for safety. COMPOUNDS of potassium are important in the CHEMISTRY of life. They are also used in fertilizers, explosives, soap and glass.

power

Power is the rate at which ENERGY is made to do work, or the rate at which one form of energy is converted to another form. The SI UNIT of energy is the joule (J). One joule used in a second equals one WATT of power. Much of the power we use comes from the COMBUSTION of PETROCHEMICALS. Electrical power can also be made from the energy of wind or waves. Dams across tidal rivers have been used to make tidal power. These sources do not pollute.

▶ Light bulbs change electrical energy into light and heat. A light bulb that does this at the rate of 60 joules per second is given a power rating of 60 watts.

▼ Some of the immense power carried by waves in the sea can be changed into useful electrical energy by floats called ducks.

precipitation

Precipitation occurs when a fluid (a liquid or gas) forms as visible PARTICLES. When the water vapour in AIR turns back to drops of water to form RAIN, we have precipitation. Adding soda to hard WATER removes CALCIUM salts, causing them to form a cloudy precipitate of particles.

▲ Water condensing in clouds may fall as rain, snow, sleet or hail depending on the temperature of the air. These are all forms of precipitation.

pressure

Pressure is a measure of how hard a force is pressing on a surface.

printing

The printing process makes many copies of text and pictures from a single original. Early methods of printing used letters (or drawings) that were higher than their background. Modern methods use a smooth printing plate. The unprinted (white) areas of the plate are kept moist, which stops ink from sticking. The areas which are to be printed are kept dry, so the ink clings on. The ink is transferred to paper as the plates roll over it.

prism

Prisms are triangular blocks of GLASS. LIGHT passing through a prism is broken into its seven COLOURS.

propane

Propane is a gas which can be DISTILLED when PETROCHEMICALS are refined. Under PRESSURE it becomes a liquid which can be stored in metal 'bottles' for use as fuel. See **plastics**.

proton

The proton is a PARTICLE found in the nucleus of an ATOM. It is like a NEUTRON but a proton has a positive charge. A neutron has no ELECTRIC charge.

▶ A printed image is made from minute dots in only four colours. Together they give an impression that many more colours and shades are present.

▶ Colour printing uses normally four colours of ink. A full colour image is built up from four different images printed one after another in yellow, magenta, cyan and black.

yellow plate — magenta plate — cyan plate — black plate

ink rollers

printing plate

paper

pulsar

P

pulsar

Pulsars are pulsating STARS. They give out RADIATION in pulses, usually about one pulse a second. Pulsars are believed to be spinning NEUTRON stars. Each pulsar weighs about as much as our SUN, but can be only ten kilometres across. This means that the DENSITY of a pulsar is very high.

▲ As a pulsar spins, it sends a beam of light sweeping through space. When the beam hits Earth the pulsar seems to flash on, and then off again as the star spins round.

pyrex

If normal glass is heated the hottest part becomes slightly larger than cooler parts. Because of this uneven EXPANSION the glass may break. Pyrex is a special kind of GLASS that has about one-tenth of the silica (silicon dioxide) replaced with boron oxide. It expands much less when it is heated. This helps to protect it from cracking, so it is ideal for cooking and for use in laboratories.

DID YOU KNOW?

Boron is used to produce pyrex, a heat-resistant glass. Other elements produce coloured glass. Cobalt turns it blue, manganese – violet, silver – yellow, iron – brown, gold – red and iridium – black. White glass is made by adding calcium fluoride, aluminium oxide or zinc oxide.

quark

Quarks are the smaller particles inside each of the protons and neutrons of an ATOM. They are 'glued' together by forces called gluons.

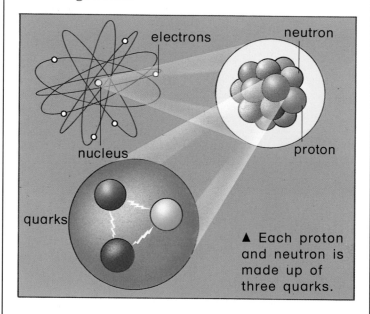

▲ Each proton and neutron is made up of three quarks.

quartz

Many of the crystals that you find in rocks at the sea-shore, or on mountains, are made of quartz. Quartz is silicon dioxide and its formula is SiO_2. Crystals of quartz are PIEZOELECTRIC.

quasar

Quasars are huge galaxies at the edge of space. They are millions of times brighter than normal galaxies, but much smaller.

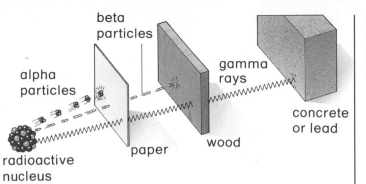

▲ Alpha particles are stopped by a thin sheet of paper. Beta particles are stopped by wood. Gamma rays are the most penetrating.

radar

Radar is a system for measuring the position of distant objects, such as ships or AIRCRAFT. Microwaves are sent out from an aerial. The REFLECTIONS from distant objects are picked up and used to show their position. See **microwave**.

radiation see pages 114 and 115

radio

Radio waves are a form of electromagnetic RADIATION. The shortest radio waves measure about one millimetre, and the longest may measure 100 kilometres.

radioactivity

Radioactivity describes the RADIATION given off by nuclear materials. In 1899 the British physicist Professor Ernest Rutherford found there were three types of radiation given off. He called them alpha, beta and gamma rays. Alpha rays are HELIUM nuclei. Beta rays are beams of ELECTRONS or POSITRONS. Gamma rays have a wavelength shorter than x-rays, and can penetrate further.

▼ To transmit music on radio, the electrical signal from the studio microphones is combined with a radio wave, called a carrier wave. This is broadcast from a radio transmitter. The combined signal is picked up by a radio aerial and decoded to create the original sound.

RADIATION

There are two types of radiation, radioactivity and electromagnetic radiation. There are many types of electromagnetic radiation, with enormous differences in wavelength. The longest radio wavelength is many kilometres. Radiation from a lightning flash makes your radio crackle. Ultraviolet makes your skin darken. X-rays can shine right through your soft tissues. We can only see a tiny part of the whole range. This we call 'light'!

RADIO WAVES

The shortest radio waves lie next to microwaves. The shorter the wavelength, the clearer the sound that a radio transmission can carry. But longer wavelengths are less likely to be reflected by hills and buildings. UHF (FM) are very short waves. They are used for radio and TV broadcasting. Radio waves are also used in cellular telephones.

MICROWAVES

Microwaves are a type of electromagnetic radiation that can pass through many solid objects but are reflected by metal. Microwaves lie between heat rays (infrared) and radio waves. They are produced by a device called a magnetron. A microwave oven uses microwaves to heat food. Microwaves are also used in radar.

ULTRAVIOLET

Ultraviolet radiation lies beyond violet light. The shortest ultraviolet rays are close to x-rays. The longer ultraviolet rays help make vitamin D in the skin, and are used to treat people with vitamin D deficiency. The shorter rays are dangerous. The ozone layer protects the Earth from much of the ultraviolet radiation from the Sun.

microwaves
(short radio waves)

radio waves

long wavelength
(low frequency)

◄ Sunbathing exposes your skin to ultraviolet (UV) radiation. Longer UV wavelengths help make vitamin D in the skin. But short UV rays damage the skin.

short wavelength (high frequency)

wavelength

gamma rays

ultraviolet

X-rays

▼ Radioactive materials are all around us. Even some our food gives us radiation. This symbol is displayed wherever radioactive substances are used.

X-RAYS

X-rays lie beyond ultraviolet. They can pass right through soft body tissues, so they can be used to see the bones inside your body. X-rays can harm living tissues, so doses are always kept to a minimum. Staff who operate x-ray machines use lead screens to protect them from too much radiation.

visible light

infrared

INFRARED

Infrared radiation lies between red light and microwaves. Infrared radiation is heat. Though we cannot see infrared we can feel the rays from a fire on our skin as heat.

LIGHT

Light rays form a very narrow band of radiation with a wavelength between 0.4 and 0.8 thousandths of a millimetre. These rays reflect from solid surfaces and are bent by lenses. This allows our eyes to focus light rays, and see the objects around us.

GAMMA RAYS

Gamma rays have the shortest wavelengths of all – they are measured in millionths of a millimetre. These rays can penetrate deeply into solid materials, and so they are used to obtain pictures of the inside of metal structures, to check for faults. Gamma rays are highly dangerous to living cells. They are used to kill cancer cells in the human body.

R

radio astronomy

Radio astronomy is the study of radio waves from space. STARS can give out RADIO WAVES more powerfully than LIGHT. Other objects may look dark, but give out strong radio signals. Radio TELESCOPES can detect the source of these waves, even if the object is too far away, or too dim to be seen with a normal telescope. NEBULAE, PULSARS and QUASARS are strong radio transmitters. Telescopes which detect other forms of RADIATION, such as X-rays or gamma rays are also used.

▼ The dish of a radio telescope collects radio signals from space and concentrates them onto an aerial positioned above the dish.

radium

Radium is a radioactive ELEMENT. COMPOUNDS of radium are always one or two degrees warmer than their surroundings because of this nuclear action. Radium was the first radioactive material to be discovered in 1898, by Pierre and Marie Curie. When Pierre was killed in a road accident Marie carried on the research alone. In later life she became ill because of all the harmful radiation she had experienced.

radon

Like radium, radon is also radioactive. But radon is a gas. It seeps out of rocks underground. In areas where there is granite in the ground, it can collect in people's homes.

rain

Rain is a type of PRECIPITATION, formed when the TEMPERATURE is above freezing. The water vapour in the air condenses into tiny droplets around dust particles, forming clouds. When the droplets are large enough, they fall as rain.

rainbow

You see a rainbow when you look into rain with the Sun behind you. Each raindrop acts like a PRISM. As sunlight bounces off the inside of the raindrop it is split into the colours of the spectrum.

▼ A rainbow is caused by sunlight which is reflected and refracted by rain drops. The Sun must be behind you in order to see the rainbow.

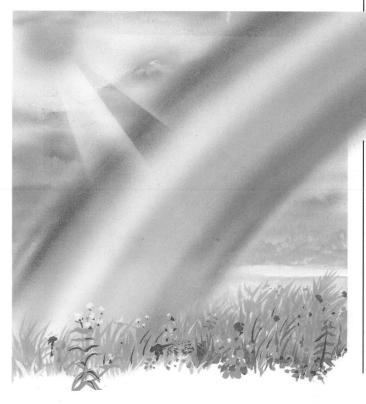

recording see **pages 118 and 119**

recycling see **page 121**

red giant
A red giant is a huge, old STAR, cooler and far larger than our SUN.

reflection
A reflection is an image of an object formed in a MIRROR. The image looks as if it had been projected straight on to the mirror. If the mirror is distorted, so is the reflection. SOUND waves and other forms of RADIATION can be reflected off surfaces.

refraction
LIGHT travels at a different VELOCITY in different substances. This causes the light rays to bend. This is refraction. LENSES refract light, as light rays travel more slowly through glass.

◄ Straws in a glass of water appear to be bent because the water refracts, or bends, light reflected from the bottom of the straws.

insulated casing

condenser

evaporator

radiator vanes give off heat

thermostat

compressor pressurizes coolant

▲ In the evaporator, heat from inside the refrigerator changes a liquid into a gas. The gas is then pumped to the condenser and compressed back to a liquid.

refrigerator
When a liquid changes to a gas it takes in ENERGY. When it cools back to a liquid, the energy is given out again. These two effects are used to keep a refrigerator cool. A liquid refrigerant is pumped through pipes in the refrigerator. It absorbs heat from the inside and turns into a gas. The gas is compressed back to a liquid in the condenser and the heat is released at the back of the refrigerator. The liquid is then pumped back inside to be used again.

relativity
The theory of relativity was developed by Albert Einstein. He proved that space and time are interchangeable, and that time on an object passes more slowly the faster the object is travelling. This can only be detected on objects moving at almost the speed of LIGHT. The theory also shows that MATTER can be converted into ENERGY. The famous equation $E = mc^2$ shows that mass (m) multiplied by the speed of light (c) squared, produces energy (E). A tiny bit of matter makes a lot of energy.

RECORDING

Recording means making a long-lasting version of something that is over very quickly. The word is usually taken to mean a sound recording. Our ears detect sound vibrations. They are heard – and gone – in a fraction of a second. Making a recording is a way of permanently storing the sound. There are three main forms of storage. One is on a vinyl record. The second is on magnetic tape. The third method of recording is on a compact disc, which can be scanned by a laser.

HI-FI SYSTEMS

A stack system has a radio, turntable for vinyl discs, a CD unit and a cassette unit below. Some hi-fis have a second cassette.

COMPACT DISCS

Tiny pits embossed in a layer of aluminium on a compact disc record a digital sound signal. A laser scans the disc.

laser beam

pit

record player

power button

compact disc

radio

graphic equalizer

cassette deck

TAPE CASSETTES

Tape cassettes are used for analogue recordings, and also for high-quality DAT (digital audio tape). Signals are stored as magnetic impulses on the tape. The tape is drawn past the head by a pinch-wheel at a carefully controlled speed.

old recording

random particles

recording head

erase head

particles in sequence

118

stylus

two tracks
give stereo
sound

groove
on record

DID YOU KNOW?

The first recording of human speech was made by Thomas Edison in 1877. He said the words: 'Mary had a little lamb'. The first tape recording was patented in Denmark in 1898. The long-playing (LP) vinyl disc was first sold in 1948. Vinyl records have now started to go out of production. They are being replaced by CDs.

VINYL RECORDS

The groove on an LP is a copy of the sound wave made at the time of the recording. The stylus moves in two directions, to give separate signals for the two speakers.

LOUDSPEAKERS

The loudspeaker changes the electrical signals (from the CD, disc or cassette) back into sound. The speaker producing low notes is the 'woofer'; high notes are recreated by the smaller 'tweeter'.

magnet

cone

coil

RECORDING SOUND

diaphragm

magnet

metal
coil

Sound waves set the diaphragm in a microphone vibrating and an electric current is created in the metal coil.

DIGITAL RECORDING

A digital recording system breaks the smooth sound wave down into separate bits of information. The sound wave is 'sampled' against a grid. Each point on the wave is given a digital value. The digital code is stored, and is used to make a recording.

analogue
signal

signal
converted
to digital
(binary)
information

01001011

digital
sampler

resonance

An object vibrates if it moves back and forth. A series of 'pushes' at exactly the right time makes the vibration stronger. This is resonance. You can see it work in a playground. If you push a swing once as it starts each swing forward, it will go higher and higher.

Richter Scale

The Richter scale measures the strength of an earthquake. Each number up the scale represents an earthquake ten times more powerful than the previous one. The scale was invented by Charles Richter, an American geologist.

rivers

When rain falls on mountains or high ground some of it soaks into the ground until it meets a layer of rock. This is groundwater. When the ground is

▼ The course of a river changes as the water carves new channels through the ground. Bends in the river sometimes form ox-bow lakes.

river valley

oxbow lake

meander

flood plain

delta

waterlogged the rainwater runs down the slope and forms a small stream. The stream collects more water off the slopes as it flows down, and joins with other streams. Eventually a river is formed. The river slowly cuts a valley out of the mountain by EROSION as it flows down the slope. As the river flows over the flatter ground towards the coast it becomes wider and slower and then eventually empties out into the ocean.

mechanical hand

▲ Robots are often used in factories to carry out a precise series of operations. Their actions are controlled by a computer program.

robot

A robot is a machine that can carry out movements which look like those of a living animal (or human). The MOVEMENTS are produced by little pumps or levers. These actions are controlled by a COMPUTER. Robots are widely used in factories, to make cars, for example.

rock

Rock is a hard substance found in the EARTH's crust. Stones and sand are broken pieces of rock. Many rocks are made up of MINERAL grains.

RECYCLING

In nature, waste materials are regularly recycled, keeping the system balanced. Modern society throws unwanted items away. This is a waste of useful resources. Recycled goods take less energy to produce than items made from raw materials, so recycling saves energy and resources.

▼ A large proportion of our domestic rubbish consists of paper and card, which can easily be recycled. Vegetable matter comes next – this can be turned into compost for the garden.

▼ Glass, metals and plastics are valuable materials which end up on the rubbish tip. They could be reclaimed and reused. There is very little in our waste that could not be put to use.

- paper and cardboard
- vegetable matter
- plastics
- textiles
- glass
- dust and cinders
- other
- metals

R

Layers of garbage in a tip are covered with clay or soil. Perforated pipes collect the methane gas produced as the waste decays. The methane can be used to provide power.

clay

soil

pipes

clay or plastics

▶ Some towns have a policy for recycling waste. People separate out aluminium cans, glass bottles and newspapers for recycling. But only one percent of our rubbish is recycled. We each throw away a kilogram of rubbish every day!

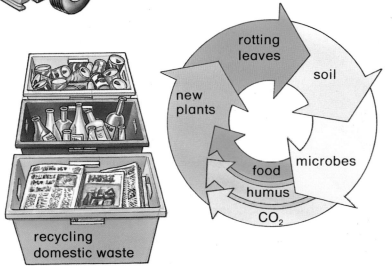

recycling domestic waste

rotting leaves

soil

new plants

microbes

food

humus

CO_2

◀ In nature, a waste material from one form of life becomes food for the next in line. When a plant dies it is broken down into its basic components by tiny organisms in the soil. These raw materials are taken up by other forms of life. In this way the chemicals are recycled through the system.

121

R

rocket

The simplest rockets are fireworks. These were first used by the Ancient Chinese, almost 1000 years ago. Inside a rocket is a FUEL and an OXYGEN source. As the fuel burns it expands and produces PRESSURE on the inside of the rocket. The pressure on the front of the rocket is not balanced by pressure at the tail, because the bottom is open and the hot gases can escape. As a result, a jet of gas is created at the tail and the rocket is forced upwards. Firework rockets use a solid fuel, like GUNPOWDER. For better control, a rocket needs liquid fuel so that the supply can be turned on or off. The first liquid fuel rocket was launched in 1926 by Robert Goddard, in Massachusetts, USA. Modern space rockets are built in sections, or stages, each with its own engine and fuel supply. The first stage is huge, and is used to push the rocket off the ground. The next stage carries the rocket out of the Earth's atmosphere, and the third stage gives the rocket enough speed to go into ORBIT. The rocket drops the first two stages when their fuel has been used up.

V2 (Germany 1944)

Long March III (China 1984)

Ariane (Europe 1981)

Apollo-Saturn (USA 1968)

US Shuttle (1981)

Vostok (USSR 1961)

Mercury-Atlas (USA 1962)

◀ Thousands of satellites have been launched by rockets since the beginning of the space age in 1957. Until 1981, rockets were used only once. The US Space Shuttle was the first spacecraft that could be used again.

Energya (USSR 1987)

rubber

Rubber is a bouncy, elastic substance. Natural rubber is extracted from the rubber tree. Synthetic rubbers are PLASTICS made from PETROCHEMICALS. Natural soft rubber can be made to react with SULPHUR to strengthen it.

rubber tree

rubber sheets

rolling

drying

▲ Natural rubber begins its life as latex collected from rubber trees. It is then thickened by adding acid or sulphur, rolled into sheets and dried.

rust

Rust forms when IRON reacts with OXYGEN and WATER. Then, the iron forms a flaky brownish crust of iron oxide. This is a form of corrosion. Iron ORE in the Earth's crust is iron combined with oxygen. In an ironworks, the oxygen is removed to leave us with pure iron. So when rust forms, the iron is returning to its original state. Stainless steel is an iron ALLOY containing CHROMIUM which does not rust.

▼ The steel in a car's body reacts with moist air to form rust. Cars are therefore covered with a protective coat of paint. If this is damaged, the car begins to rust.

S

salt

Common salt, which we use in cooking, is sodium chloride, a COMPOUND containing the atoms of SODIUM and CHLORINE. Salt is important for keeping the body healthy. There are many other chemical salts. All ACIDS contain HYDROGEN, and if the hydrogen atom is replaced with a METAL atom a salt is formed. Sodium chloride can be produced when an acid containing chlorine (hydrogen chloride) reacts with an alkali containing sodium (sodium hydroxide). See **acid and alkali**.

litmus paper

acid (hydrogen chloride)

base (sodium hydroxide)

salt (sodium chloride)

water

▲ The reaction to produce common salt is shown above. Water is the by-product of the reaction and is evaporated to obtain the salt crystals.

▲ Artificial satellites relay telephone calls and television programmes around the world. They also record the world's changing weather and collect information for scientists.

satellite
Satellites are small bodies which are in ORBIT around larger ones. The Moon orbits the Earth. It is the Earth's natural satellite. In 1957, the USSR launched the first artificial satellite, *Sputnik 1*, which orbited the Earth. Since then many other satellites have been launched. The most important uses of satellites are surveying the Earth, helping ships and planes to navigate and to transmit RADIO and TELEVISION signals from one country to another.

Saturn
Saturn is the sixth planet, famous for its rings, and the farthest planet known to ancient astronomers. It is big enough to contain 752 planets the size of our EARTH. See **Solar System**.

seismograph
A seismograph is used to measure MOVEMENTS of the EARTH. It has a large weight on a bar suspended by a spring. As the Earth trembles in an EARTHQUAKE, the weight has enough INERTIA to keep still while the rest of the equipment moves. A pen traces the movements onto paper.

▼ Seismographs measure the shock waves produced by an earthquake. Both horizontal and vertical movements of the Earth's crust are measured. A pen traces out the pattern of movement on a roll of paper.

spring

pen

drum

vertical movement

sideways movement

semiconductor
Semiconductors are special minerals that allow the ELECTRONS that produce an ELECTRIC CURRENT to flow in one direction, but not in the opposite direction. The action of some semiconductors can be switched by an electric charge. A large number of semiconductors can be made into a COMPUTER. The way they control and switch the flow of electricity enables computers to store data and make calculations at high speed. See **transistor**.

SHADOWS

Shadows form when solid objects block the light. Your own body casts a shadow on a sunny day. A rain-shadow is the area of land downwind from a line of hills. The rain falls on the hills, and the rain-shadow area has little rainfall. Television 'shadows' are areas where a TV signal is screened off by mountains and reception is poor.

▶ The length of a shadow depends on the angle between the Sun and the ground. In the tropics near midday the Sun is overhead, and people stand in their own shadows. Away from the tropics the Sun is in the east at 6 am, and in the west at 6 pm. At midday it is to the south. If you remember this you can always tell which direction you are facing when the Sun is shining.

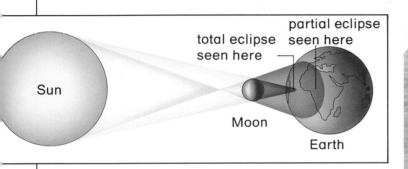

total eclipse seen here

partial eclipse seen here

Sun

Moon

Earth

▲ The Moon sometimes blocks out the Sun and its shadow falls on the Earth. We see a solar eclipse. The whole scene goes as dark as night until the Sun peeks past the Moon again. If the Moon is on the far side of the Earth, the Earth's shadow can fall on the Moon and the Moon disappears. This is a lunar eclipse.

▼ Shadows can be used in theatre. There is a strong tradition of shadow puppets in Thailand, for example. You can cut paper shapes to produce shadow puppets, and even your hands can make many animals. Rabbits, dogs and even a flying bird are easy to make and use to illustrate a story.

chicken's head   rabbit's head   flying bird   dog's head

S

SI units

SI stands for Système International. It describes the international system of units of MEASUREMENT which is used by scientists around the world. There are seven basic units, each of which has a standard definition. For example, the standard kilogram is a cylinder of a platinum ALLOY. SI units have been used since 1960.

unit name and symbol	physical quantity	
metre (m)	length	
kilogram (kg)	mass	
second (s)	time	
ampere (a)	electric current	
Kelvin (K)	thermodynamic temperature	
candela (cd)	luminous intensity	
mole (mol)	amount of substance	

▲ These are the seven basic SI units. All other units used in science and technology, such as watts and joules, stem from these basic units.

silver

Silver is a white, shiny, precious metal. It is quite soft, but does not react with OXYGEN, so it stays beautifully shiny a long time. Silver eventually turns black, because it reacts with sulphur gases in the air to form silver sulphide, which is dark.

siphon

Water can sometimes flow uphill. It flows *up* a pipe, if the far end of the pipe is hanging below the surface of the water. You can siphon a liquid from one

◀ A straw in a carton of juice can act as a siphon. If the end of the straw dips below the level of the juice, it may run out.

container by sucking it up into a tube, and placing the end of the tube in another container lower down. The water will flow into the second container until the level of liquid is the same as that in the first.

soap

Soaps are alkali SALTS of fatty ACIDS (MOLECULES found in animal fat and plant OIL). Soaps made with POTASSIUM are soft. Soaps of SODIUM are hard, and soaps of other metals do not dissolve in WATER. Soaps lift dirt from skin and clothing.

sodium

Sodium is a soft white METAL. It is very reactive, and it burns if it comes in contact with WATER. Sodium is used in NUCLEAR REACTORS to carry heat. Your body needs a little sodium to stay healthy.

software

Software is the name given to the programs that you run in a COMPUTER. The machinery is the hardware.

▲ The solar panels on this car trap sunlight energy and use it to make electricity to power the car. Solar energy does not cause pollution.

solar energy

Most ENERGY comes from the Sun. Humans are powered by this stored energy, when they eat food. A COAL fire is releasing ancient solar energy, too. Modern solar cells collect sunlight and turn it straight into electricity. They provide solar power for SPACECRAFT. Solar cells have also been used for small cars.

Solar System see **pages 128 and 129**

sonar

Sonar is like RADAR. But instead of using RADIO waves, sonar uses ULTRASOUND. A 'ping' is sent out by a ship and its ECHO is recorded. COMPUTERS measure the time between the sound and the echo to work out how far away an object is.

▼ Sonar is used by ships to measure water depth. The seabed is shown on a TV screen.

sound see **page 131**

sound barrier

Sound waves move away from an aircraft in all directions. If the plane is flying at the speed of SOUND it catches up with the sound waves. They build up in front of the plane as a shock wave – known as 'the sound barrier'. Planes flying faster than sound leave a loud bang, called a sonic boom, behind them. It is caused as the plane breaks through the sound barrier and the shock waves reach the ground.

Galileo

Giotto

Viking

Venera

▲ *Giotto* was the first spacecraft to fly alongside a comet, Halley's Comet, in 1986. *Venera* landed on Venus, *Viking* searched for life on Mars and *Galileo* is the latest spacecraft to visit Jupiter.

spacecraft

Spacecraft are objects designed to fly through space. They include SATELLITES launched by a rocket into ORBIT around the EARTH, and vehicles which travel far into the SOLAR SYSTEM to send back information about the PLANETS.

SOLAR SYSTEM

The Solar System measures twelve billion kilometres from one side to the other. It consists of nine planets which orbit the Sun, plus millions of asteroids, meteors and comets. Most of the planets have moons of their own. The surface of the Sun is covered with waves of hot gas. Some project out from the surface. These huge flames are often larger than the Earth.

DID YOU KNOW?

Most of the planets are named after the gods of ancient times. Mars was the god of war, and Venus the goddess of love and peace. Mercury was the winged messenger of the gods, and Saturn was the ancient god of farming. Saturn was the outermost planet known to the ancient world. Jupiter was lord of them all. Pluto, the outermost planet known, was discovered in 1930. Its orbit sometimes brings it closer to the Earth than Neptune. There may be another planet beyond Pluto!

Sun

Mercury

Venus

Earth

Mars

Jupiter

Planet	Distance from Sun	Number of Moons	Diameter	Interesting Facts
Mercury	58 million km	None	4878 km	Its year lasts only 88 Earth days
Venus	108 million km	None	12,100 km	The hottest planet, hidden by clouds.
Earth	150 million km	1	12,756 km	The only planet known to have air, water and life.
Mars	228 million km	2	6790 km	The 'red planet' is named after its dusty red surface.
Jupiter	778 million km	16	142,700 km	A day only lasts about 10 Earth hours.
Saturn	1427 million km	24	120,000 km	Its famous rings measure over 300,000 km across.
Uranus	2870 million km	15	50,000 km	The first planet discovered with a telescope.
Neptune	4497 million km	8	50,000 km	Its year lasts 165 Earth years.
Pluto	5900 million km	1	3000 km	Forty times as far from the Sun as the Earth is.

JUPITER'S RED SPOT

A gigantic swirling mass of red gas that can be seen near the equator of Jupiter is known as the Great Red Spot. It was first seen over 300 years ago when primitive telescopes were used. Jupiter also has a smaller 'yellow spot'.

ASTEROIDS AND RING SYSTEMS

Between Mars and Jupiter there is a belt of rocky bodies called asteroids. They range up to 1000 kilometres in size. Some, like Eros, have passed quite close to Earth. Saturn became famous for its giant ring system when Galileo discovered it with his new telescope in the early 1600s. In recent years other ring systems have been found. There is even a very fine ring around Jupiter.

Neptune

Pluto

Saturn

Uranus

S

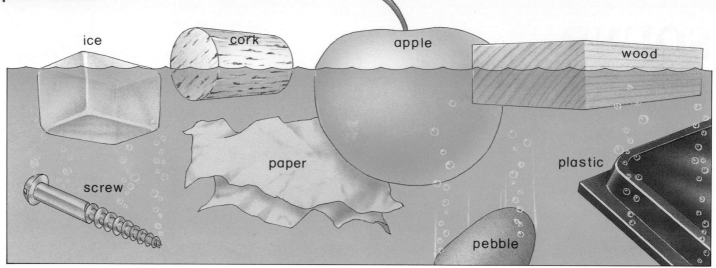

ice
cork
apple
wood
screw
paper
plastic
pebble

Space Shuttle

The Space Shuttle is a special SPACECRAFT which can be sent into space and then land back on Earth like a plane. The Shuttle can be used for many flights whereas normal ROCKETS can be used only once. The first Shuttle was *Columbia*, which was launched by the US in 1981. *Buran* was built in Russia and this was followed by the construction of *Hermes* in Europe. Shuttles are also being designed in Germany, India and Japan.

▲ Ice, apples and most woods have a specific gravity lower than that of water, so they float. Stone and most metals have a specific gravity which is higher than water's, so they sink.

specific gravity

Specific gravity is the MASS of a volume of any substance compared with the mass of the same volume of WATER. Something with a specific gravity of more than 1.0 has a greater DENSITY than water, and sinks. Less than 1.0 and it has a lower density, and floats. Specific gravity is now termed relative density.

satellite
manned-manoeuvring unit
robot arm
payload bay
flight deck
spacelab
rest room

◀ The Space Shuttle can carry satellites into space and collect faulty satellites for repair. The crew works in the craft's nose section. A laboratory may be carried in the cargo bay and is linked to the nose section by a tunnel.

SOUND

Sound waves are vibrations that travel through a medium (which can be solid, liquid or gas). They cannot travel in a vacuum so they will not travel across space. Space is silent! Sound waves travel out in a spreading circle, getting weaker (so the sound becomes quieter) the farther they go. Sound waves are a bit like ripples in a pond.

Sound travels millions of times slower than light, so it can take a while before the sound of a distant explosion reaches you. Watch someone burst a balloon or bang a piece of wood at the far end of the street, and you will see the action a split second before you hear it.

DID YOU KNOW?

The speed of sound at sea level is about 1200 km/h. At high altitudes it is 1060 km/h. Sound travels three times as fast through helium, and four times as fast in hydrogen.

hydrogen
1360 metres
per second

helium
1020 metres
per second

air
340
metres
per
second

water
1500 metres
per second

glass
4500 metres
per second

distance travelled in one second

cat
65,000

dog
50,000

human
20,000

70
60
50
1000 Hertz
40
30
20
10

hearing range

◀ Animals can hear sounds that are higher than we can detect. Cats can hear sounds with a frequency of up to 65 kHz. Dogs have an upper range of 50 kHz. Young people can hear up to 20 kHz.

131

steam

flywheel

piston

cylinder   piston   driving
            rod   rod

◀ Inside a steam engine, steam is directed in front of the piston and then behind it to push it back and forth. This is then changed into a rotating motion to turn the wheels of a vehicle such as a steam locomotive.

star see **page 133**

static
Static is a form of ELECTRICITY. LIGHTNING is a form of static in the atmosphere. You can see sparks of static when you take off an acrylic jumper at night.

boiler   firebox   fire doors

chimney

piston

crank

stalactites and stalagmites
Stalactites and stalagmites are spiky deposits of calcium that form in limestone caves. As rainwater drips through the caves, the dissolved calcium is deposited and builds up into tall stone spikes.

▼ Stalactites hang down from the cave's ceiling. Stalagmites grow from the ground upwards. And sometimes they meet in the middle.

water wears
away rock
limestone

caves

stalactites

stalagmites

steam
Steam is the vapour produced when WATER BOILS. It contains much stored ENERGY, and can easily scald people. A steam engine uses steam to push a piston. It produces high POWER even when turning very slowly because it generates most TORQUE at low speeds. Modern engines have to turn over at high speed to produce most energy.

steel
Steel is made by adding a small amount of CARBON to IRON. It is harder than iron but still rusts. Stainless steel contains CHROMIUM to protect it from CORROSION.

stereo
Stereophonic or 'stereo' RECORDINGS are made with separate tracks for the sound heard by each ear.

STARS

Stars are massive luminous bodies in space. You can see 5780 stars with an unaided eye. But some stars are invisible, and emit radiation in wavelengths we cannot see. Many of the bright objects in the night sky are not stars, but whole galaxies. The nearest star to us is called the Sun. It is half-way through its life-cycle and will last another five billion years.

▼ Our own star, the Sun, is halfway through its life. Inside it is a giant nuclear reactor powered by fusion. The Sun is about 80 percent hydrogen and 20 percent helium.

Sun as it is today

Stars are born when a nebula collapses and star clusters develop from the remains. There is enough hydrogen inside to fuel the star for thousands of millions of years. As the hydrogen fuel is used up, the Sun will expand into a red giant and engulf the Earth. The shell of hot gas will be blown away leaving a white dwarf. After billions of years it will cool down and form a black dwarf – a dead star.

star grows

star runs out of hydrogen and expands

nebula collapses

matter condenses and forms a protostar

black dwarf

star cools

white dwarf

young stars are born

star condenses

centre of star shrinks and forms a planetary nebula

red giant

star burns helium and expands further

stratosphere

This is the thin second layer of the atmosphere. It starts about 15 kilometres above the ground. This is where supersonic AIRCRAFT such as Concorde fly.

strobe

A strobe is a flash of LIGHT that makes a moving object appear still. This effect is seen when a moving object is glimpsed for a split second. A flashing light in a disco seems to freeze a moving dancer. In some Western films for the CINEMA, the wagon wheels seem to turn backwards. This strobe effect is seen as the spokes nearly catch each other up in the time between each separate frame.

prominence

sunspot

◄ At the centre of the Sun, hydrogen is changed into helium. Heat and light are released. Vast tongues of gas called solar flares fly into space from its surface.

—chromosphere

photosphere

—core

◄ Wagon wheels seem to turn backwards on film because of the strobe effect. A film is made up of a series of still frames. Note the position of spoke a in frame 1.

◄ In the time between each frame, the wheels continue to turn. In the second frame spoke b has moved almost to where spoke a was originally.

◄ To your eye it looks as though the spokes have moved back a little in each frame, and it appears that the wheels are turning backwards.

Sun

The Sun is an ordinary, and not very important, STAR. At least, that's how it would seem to any alien scientist! It is important to us, because it is our source of ENERGY. The Sun is 150 million kilometres from the Earth. It is a huge nuclear reactor. In its centre, the temperature is about 14 million°C. The surface is at 6000°C. Cooler areas show through, as sunspots. They can sometimes be seen when the Sun is setting. (*Never* use binoculars or a telescope to look at the Sun. The heat energy is dangerous.)

supernova

A supernova is a massive nova produced by the collapse of a giant STAR. A small NEUTRON STAR is usually formed when the supernova has ended.

flying below the speed of sound

aircraft reaches the speed of sound

flying above the speed of sound

shock wave

sonic boom heard here

supersonic

Supersonic planes travel faster than the speed of sound. Because of the air friction, they get hot on the outside. The windows of Concorde become too hot to touch. See **Mach**.

surface tension

The molecules of water pull each other in all directions. At the surface they are only pulled back towards the other water MOLECULES and this makes a kind of skin. The effect is known as surface tension.

▶ Surface tension pulls a droplet of water into a spherical (ball) shape. Surface tension is also strong enough to allow an insect called a pond skater to glide on top of the water without falling in.

pond skater

▲ Sound waves spread out from a plane flying below the speed of sound. As it nears the speed of sound, it catches up with its own sound waves. As it passes the speed of sound, they form a shock wave, heard as a sonic boom.

suspension

PARTICLES that are very tiny can stay suspended in a liquid for a long time. Milk is a suspension of fat in water. A suspension is the liquid version of an AEROSOL.

synthesizer see **page 136**

synthetic

A synthetic product is one that people make. A natural product is one that occurs in nature. Synthetic products are often based on natural ones, for instance many drugs were first found in plants.

DID YOU KNOW?

Many synthetic materials were discovered by accident. Polythene was first made when the apparatus sprang a leak. Modern dyes were discovered by accident, during research on quinine. The hardening of rubber to make tyres was a chance discovery by Charles Goodyear.

S

SYNTHESIZER

A synthesizer creates sound vibrations
that imitate musical instruments (and
other sounds). Technologists analyse
the patterns of a sound, and then
program hardware to set up the same
patterns artificially. A synthesizer can
sound like an organ or a guitar, and
some can manage a roaring
lion or a space alien as well.

The keyboard is based
on a piano keyboard.
The white notes, played
in sequence, give the
scale of C. The note of
C is always to the left of
the pair of black notes.
Groups of notes are
chords. The lower notes
of your synthesizer
probably play chords
automatically.

liquid
crystal
display

tempo

programme
(instrument)
selection

pitch
control

beat
selector

volume
control

speaker

136

▲ Synthesizers have a
range of drum beat
options, and some fill-in
phrases as well. Many
modern recordings have
been made by a single
artist, with only a
synthesizer to create the
entire sound.

▲ With practice you
may be able to recreate
some of your favourite
records on a
synthesizer. The
microchips make the
task much easier than
following the musical
score. First you need to
set the tempo (not too
fast), and select the
type of music you want
to play (for example
blues or rap). Next
choose a suitable
'voice' such as electric
guitar. Try this twelve-
bar rhythm and blues
sequence: C/C/C/C/F/
F/C/C/G/F/C/C.

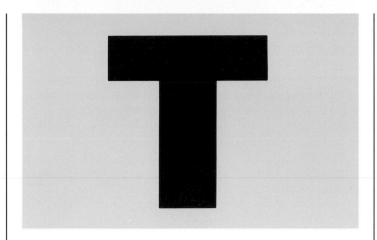

tape see **recording**

telephone

The first commercial telephone was made by Alexander Graham Bell in 1876. Modern telephones are similar to Bell's early designs. There is a MICROPHONE which picks up SOUND signals. The ELECTRICAL signal it creates is sent to a distant phone. There the signal is changed back to sound in an earpiece, and the original words can be heard.

▼ A telephone mouthpiece has a microphone which changes the speaker's voice into an electrical signal. A loudspeaker in the earpiece turns the signals back into sound.

earpiece

diaphragm

electromagnet

wire coil

microphone

mouthpiece

light

mirrors

reflecting telescope

▲ Large telescopes for studying the planets and stars magnify these distant objects by means of curved mirrors. They are called reflectors. Telescopes that use lenses instead are called refractors.

telescope

Telescopes make distant objects appear nearer. One that magnifies ten times (written 10 ×) would make an object ten kilometres away look as though it was only one kilometre away. Large telescopes have a magnifying MIRROR to enlarge the image. Smaller telescopes use LENSES to produce the magnification. The largest telescope in the world is the Kech telescope in Hawaii which has a mirror ten metres across.

television see **page 138**

TELEVISION

The first public television service started in London in 1932. It used the system invented by John Baird, and gave very blurred pictures. Modern TV pictures are built up on screen line by line. The start of public electronic television was in Berlin in 1935, with 180 lines across the screen. Clear TV pictures (with 405 lines) were transmitted from London the following year.

▼ The electronic signals from the studio are sent to a transmission station. Here they are amplified, and sent out from the transmission mast. The signal travels hundreds of kilometres.

Some television transmitters are on satellites orbiting the Earth. With no houses or mountains in the way, these signals can be broadcast over an entire continent.

▼ Light from an object is scanned by the TV camera. Modern cameras split the picture into 625 lines. Each line is converted into three sets of signals – one each for red, blue and green – the primary colours of light. The strength of the signal depends on the amount of each colour reflected by the object. In this case it is a vase, but it can be a newsreader or a rock star.

◄ The aerial on your roof points towards the transmitter. It picks up the signal, which is strengthened by an amplifier. The signal is then split into its three parts. The three signals are sent as beams of electrons (cathode rays) to the screen, where they are focused on coloured phosphors. The phosphors glow brightly when a signal hits them. If you look closely at a TV screen you can see how the picture is built up.

radio waves

transmission mast

transmission station

video signal

aerial

encoder

primary colour signals

camera

amplifier

camera tube

electron beams

mirror

electron guns

phosphors

temperature

Temperature measures how hot something is. Traditionally temperature was measured in degrees Fahrenheit, with the freezing point of water at 32°F and its boiling point at 212°F. The CELSIUS scale was then adopted, with freezing at 0°C and boiling at 100°C. The Kelvin is the SI UNIT for temperature. Degrees Kelvin are the same size as degrees CELSIUS, but the scale begins at ABSOLUTE ZERO (0 K or −273.16°C), which is the point at which molecules can be cooled no further. Water freezes at 273 K.

	Celsius	Fahrenheit
freezing point (0°C)	**0**	**32**
	10	50
	20	68
	30	86
	40	104
	50	122
	60	140
	70	158
	80	176
	90	194
boiling point	**100**	**212**
	110	230
	120	248
	130	266
	140	284
	150	302
	200	392
	250	482
	300	572

◀ A temperature on one scale can be converted to another scale by doing a simple calculation. Multiply degrees Celsius by nine, divide it by five and add 32 to give the temperature in degrees Fahrenheit.

theodolite

Theodolites are used to measure the contours of the Earth's surface. A TELESCOPE or LASER is aimed at the top of a hill or to a distant point. The distance and angle between this and a known reference point are then read off a scale.

thermocouple

If two different metals are joined together in a loop, they may produce ELECTRICITY if one of the joins is heated. The more it is heated, the more electricity is produced. This idea can be used to measure TEMPERATURE with ELECTRICAL instruments. IRON and COPPER act as a thermocouple.

thermometer

A thermometer is a device for measuring TEMPERATURE. Some thermometers are made of glass, with a liquid inside which EXPANDS as the temperature goes up. Others contain a THERMOCOUPLE. A LIQUID CRYSTAL thermometer shows temperature by a change of colour.

▼ When a thermometer is taken out of a patient's mouth, it begins to cool down. A small kink at the bottom of the mercury channel breaks the thread of contracting mercury and stops it from falling, so an accurate reading can be taken.

DID YOU KNOW?

The highest shade temperature ever recorded was 57.7°C at Al'Aziziyah, Libya on September 13, 1922. The coldest temperature was −89.2°C at Vostok, Antarctica on July 21, 1983.

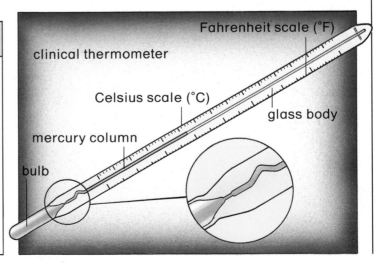

clinical thermometer

Fahrenheit scale (°F)

Celsius scale (°C)

glass body

mercury column

bulb

▶ Tomato ketchup is thixotropic. It is normally thick, but becomes thinner when the bottle is shaken.

thixotropism

Thixotropic substances are quite stiff if you leave them standing, but become runny if you move them about. This effect is known as thixotropism. Gel paints are thixotropic. They are solid until you begin painting, when they turn into a liquid and are easier to spread.

tide

Water is pulled down on the EARTH by GRAVITY. But the water in the seas and OCEANS is also pulled by the gravity of the SUN and MOON. This causes the regular rise and fall of the sea which we call the tides.

▼ High Spring tides occur when the Sun and Moon are in line with the Earth. When the Sun and Moon are at right angles to each other we get low tides called neap tides.

spring tides

neap tides

When the Sun and Moon pull together, you get very high tides. They are called Spring tides, and they are always two days after a full (or new) Moon. Neap tides are lower, and occur two weeks later, when the Sun and Moon are pulling against each other. Spring and Neap tides always seem to happen at the same time of day at any set place.

time

Time is the passing of the present into history. It is measured by comparison with natural events. A day is the time it takes the EARTH to spin round once and is

Greenwich Meridian   International Dateline

▲ The world is divided into 24 time zones. The time is one hour later in each zone to the east.

▼ In this clock, the cane burns slowly, dropping balls on the cymbal at regular intervals.

fire clock

marked by the Sun rising in the sky. A year is the time the Earth takes to make on ORBIT of the Sun. Before there were clocks and watches, people used SHADOWS or candles to tell how time was passing.

tin
Tin is a soft silvery metal. A rod of tin squeaks as you bend it, because it is made of CRYSTALS which rub together. Tin is used to coat STEEL, to stop RUST forming. It is also used to make many useful ALLOYS.

titanium
Titanium is a very hard light metal. It is present in almost all ROCKS. Titanium is a useful metal for making ALLOYS for planes and spacecraft.

tornado
A tornado is a twisting wind that moves at high speed. The AIR may travel at 500 km/h in a tornado. At the centre of the tornado, the PRESSURE of the air is very low. Buildings sometimes EXPLODE when a tornado passes over, because the air pressure inside the building is high by comparison. Tornadoes are most common in Australia and the USA.

torque
Torque is the FORCE of twisting. A screwdriver develops torque as it turns. A car engine twists, or applies torque, to the crankshaft. High performance cars have high torque engines.

transformer
A transformer is a device for changing ELECTRICITY from a high to a low VOLTAGE (or the other way round). Transformers are made by wrapping two coils of copper

▲ The way a transformer changes voltage depends on the numbers of coils of wire on each side. The transformer on the left reduces the voltage. The one on the right increases it.

wire round an IRON core. The voltage produced depends on the number of coils in each set. If the second set has twice as many coils as the first set, the voltage will be doubled. Or, if it has half as many coils as the first set, the voltage will be halved.

transistor
A transistor is a sandwich of SEMICONDUCTORS. Transistors were discovered in the USA after World War II. Many new ways were found to make semiconductors control ELECTRIC currents. They are used as switches or to amplify an electric current. They are very small and are now used in making RADIO and TELEVISION equipment.

▼ A weak electric current flowing into the middle, or base, connection of a transistor produces a larger change in the emitter-collector current.

T

trinitrotoluene

Trinitrotoluene is a very powerful EXPLOSIVE made up of carbon, nitrogen, oxygen and hydrogen. It is known as TNT for short.

tungsten

Tungsten is a very hard, brittle metal with a very high melting point (3380°C). It is used to make ALLOYS, and is also found in ELECTRIC light bulbs.

► Cutting tools are often made from a tough mixture of tungsten and carbon called tungsten carbide.

counter sink
washer
rotary cutter
drill bit

turbine

A turbine is a fan pushed round by the PRESSURE of gas or water. A JET engine is a turbine. A power station GENERATOR is often POWERED by a turbine.

▼ In this steam turbine, stationary blades direct the steam onto the turbine wheels. The fans spin round and drive the shaft.

turbine blades
fixed blades
incoming steam
rotating shaft

ultra high frequency

Ultra high frequency waves are RADIO waves between 300 and 3000 megahertz. They are known as UHF for short. UHF waves are used to broadcast TELEVISION signals. See **hertz**, **very high frequency**.

ultrasound

Ultrasound is too high for people to hear. Humans can hear SOUNDS up to 20,000 HERTZ. Anything above this is ultrasonic. Early remote control units for TELEVISION sets produced ultrasonic beams. But they frightened cats and dogs, which can hear these high notes. So remote controls now use INFRARED or RADIO signals.

ultraviolet radiation

Ultraviolet is the RADIATION that lies beyond the blue end of the COLOURS of a rainbow. Though it is invisible, many insects can see ultraviolet as LIGHT. Short wave ultraviolet rays from the Sun damage eyes and skin.

universe

The universe is the word we use to describe everything we know to exist. It includes all the STARS, the PLANETS in the SOLAR SYSTEM, and the GALAXIES. Between all these bodies is interstellar space, with a small amount of gas and dust spread very, very thinly.

▼ The Universe is mostly empty space with galaxies, stars, planets, moons, comets, asteroids, gas and dust scattered throughout it.

uranium

Uranium is a hard, white METAL. It is naturally RADIOACTIVE. There are many ISOTOPES of this ELEMENT. For example, uranium has 92 PROTONS, but between 142 and 146 NEUTRONS. This makes between 234 and 238 PARTICLES altogether in each ATOM. Uranium-238 makes up 99 percent of the natural uranium found in the ORE in rocks. Uranium-235 makes up less than one percent of the ore and is used in nuclear reactors and nuclear weapons.

Uranus

Uranus is the seventh PLANET from the SUN. It was discovered in 1781 by William Herschel, an English chapel organist who studied the SOLAR SYSTEM in his spare time. It has an almost vertical ring system.

double-walled glass bottle

screw-on lid

vacuum

silvered walls

shock absorber

◄ A partial vacuum between the inner and outer walls of a vacuum flask stops heat from flowing out and keeps the liquid inside hot. It also stops cold liquids from warming up.

vacuum

A vacuum is completely empty space. A perfect vacuum does not exist. Even out between the distant STARS there are always ATOMS and MOLECULES floating around. A vacuum cleaner, or vacuum brakes on a train, work with AIR at low PRESSURE, called a partial vacuum. A partial vacuum is created inside a vacuum cleaner, and air and dust rush in to fill it. A vacuum flask is a container with two layers of silvered glass. Most of the air between the two layers of glass is pumped out. The silvering reflects back HEAT, preventing loss of ENERGY by radiation. The 'vacuum' space prevents the heat from being conducted away. And the lid helps stop convection. The result is that your drink stays at the same temperature.

V

velocity

Velocity is speed in a certain direction. A car has velocity as it drives along a road, but a spinning wheel does not have velocity. Only things in linear motion have velocity. See **movement**.

Venus

Venus is a hot and mysterious PLANET, about the same size as EARTH but nearer to the SUN. Since 1992 Venus has been surveyed in detail by the Magellan space probe which was sent into ORBIT around it.

very high frequency

Very high frequency (VHF) waves are radio waves below ULTRA HIGH FREQUENCY. They have a frequency of about 100 megahertz.

video see **page 145**

volcano

Volcanoes are formed when molten ROCK from under the crust of the EARTH escapes through a weak point. They are often found at the joins between parts of the Earth's crust. There are 500 active volcanoes around the world, some more than 6000 metres tall. The molten rock called LAVA can flow for more than 60 kilometres. See **plate tectonics**.

volt

The volt is the SI UNIT for measuring voltage – the difference in ENERGY of two electric charges. Voltage is also called the electromotive force or potential difference. It is the FORCE that drives an electric CURRENT around a CIRCUIT. A torch BATTERY generates a force of about two volts. Mains electricity is about 240 volts, and can kill you. The volt is named after Alessandro Volta, an Italian scientist who explained potential difference.

▼ When a volcano erupts hot molten rock, called lava, pours out of the central and side vents. Layers of ash and lava build up a cone-shaped mountain. Dykes, sills and laccoliths are formed when lava hardens underground.

ash and smoke

main vent

lava

side vent

layers of ash and lava

geyser

laccolith

sill

crust

dyke

underground chamber

VIDEO

A video camera captures light and focuses the image onto a sensitive target plate. This is usually a semiconductor device. The target produces electrical signals which are stored on magnetic tape. Part of the signal is fed to a viewfinder, so you can see what the lens is seeing. The whole device – with camera and recorder in one body – is known as a camcorder.

▼ A microphone beside the lens picks up the sound. Camcorder microphones are very sensitive. A separate microphone is used for professional results.

lens

monitor

microphone

lens

light

controls

videotape

light-sensitive plate

VIDEOTAPE

The record/playback head lays down the track as a series of slanting lines on the tape. The sound-track and a time code are laid down alongside.

take-up spool

feedhead

erase head

record-playback head

close-up of tape

sound track

picture signals

time code

▲ Some camcorders are fitted with a colour view-finder. But a black-and-white screen often gives a sharper image. It is best to focus the camera lens manually, because automatic will drain the batteries very quickly.

HOME VIDEO

When you make a video, do not film the same scene for long. Always change the position of the shot before you turn the camera on again if you want to avoid a sudden jump in the action. Shoot short (called cut-aways) close-ups to break up long scenes.

waste

Waste is material that you do not need. Most of the waste from homes and factories is buried in landfill sites, or burnt in an incinerator. Many waste products are dangerous and strict laws are needed to make sure they are disposed of safely. RECYCLING is a good way to reduce the amount of waste we produce.

water see pages 148 and 149

watt

The watt is the SI UNIT of POWER. It measures the rate at which ENERGY is used up, or converted to another form. One watt represents the use of one JOULE of energy per second.

▲ The British engineer James Watt (1736–1819) improved the design of steam engines in the 1770s. The SI unit of power is named after him.

wave

A wave is a steady rise and fall, like water at sea. Wavelength is the distance from the peak of one wave to the next. The height is the distance between the peak and the trough. The power of the waves at sea can be used to generate ELECTRICITY.

▼ As waves roll onto the seashore from far out to sea, the water particles circle up and down. The water itself does not move forwards, but the wave travels towards the shore.

wavelength

peak

trough

water

anemometer

weather vane

psychrometer

thermometer

barograph

N

▲ These pieces of equipment record weather conditions of air temperature and pressure, humidity, and wind speed and direction.

▼ Annual rainfall around the world ranges from a few millimetres in desert regions to more than 3000 mm in places like the Amazon rainforest.

W

weather

Weather is the name given to the changing conditions that are the result of the SUN'S ENERGY acting on the WATER and the AIR which surround us. They include TEMPERATURE, PRECIPITATION, air pressure, HUMIDITY, sunshine, cloud cover and WIND. Near the POLES of the EARTH the air is cold. Around the Equator it is much hotter. Where the two air masses meet the weather is very changeable. The cold air can move across countries, as a cold front. Warm air can push it back, bringing a warm front. There is usually cloud and rain where the two air masses meet. Sometimes the two air masses swirl around each other, like eddies and whirlpools in a stream. These are depressions, where the PRESSURE of the air is low. Still and calm air has high pressure and is called an anticyclone. When the pressure is falling (you can see it on a BAROMETER) poor weather is likely. See **climate**, **meteorology**.

Tropic of Cancer

Equator

Tropic of Capricorn

mm

over 3000
2000–3000
1000–2000
500–1000
250–500
under 250

WATER

There are more than a billion cubic kilometres of water on our planet. At the North and South Poles it is frozen into permanent ice, and in the air it exists as colourless water vapour. Together all this water makes up seven percent of the Earth's mass. Water is made of two atoms of hydrogen bonded with one of oxygen. Its formula is H_2O. Water can dissolve more different chemicals than any other liquid known.

▼ Water exists on Earth in all three states of matter. Ice and snow on the mountains melt to water under the heat of the Sun. Vapour is given off as the water is heated up for cooking. Water is vital for life. Human bodies are two-thirds water, and some plants contain more than 90 percent.

▼ You could say that if ice sank, life would never have evolved. Life began in the sea, originally there were no living things on land. If ice did not float, the sea would freeze from the bottom up. This would mean that all the living things would have been stranded on the top and would have died.

DID YOU KNOW?

Water has an amazing property – when it freezes solid, it expands. Other liquids slowly contract as they cool. A frozen water-pipe may split because of this. Nothing happens until the ice melts – that's when you find the leak!

▲ Ice from the North and South Poles breaks off to form icebergs. The largest can be larger than Belgium! There is nine times as much of the iceberg below the surface as there is above. This is why icebergs are a danger to ships.

ice   water   steam

▲ Ice takes in a lot of energy to melt to water, just as water does to become vapour. This latent heat is given out again when vapour condenses to water, and water freezes to ice.

◀▼ Water attacks many things. A stream can dissolve away limestone, to form caves. The solid steel of a car can be attacked by water and changed to powdery rust. Even the washing of waves on the shore wears away tall cliffs.

DID YOU KNOW?

Think what happens when you hang a tee-shirt over a radiator to dry. The radiator heats the tee-shirt and evaporates the water. You can see the window misting as the vapour condenses on the cold glass.

▲ Freezing the water in food keeps it fresh, because the microorganisms which spoil food cannot grow without liquid water.

▲ Inside a seed is a plant embryo. When water is added, the embryo grows and bursts out of the seed case. Try growing some seeds in a pot, and watch water at work.

149

rollers
over 5000 years ago

solid wooden wheels
5000 years ago

potters wheel
3250 BC

water wheel
Middle Ages

spoked wheel
19th century

▲ The invention of the wheel 5000 years ago led to the development of vehicles and machines of many different kinds.

weight

Weight is a measure of how heavy something is. A ten kilogram weight always has a MASS of ten kilograms; but on the MOON it will weigh only 1.7 kilograms. This is because the force of GRAVITY is only one-sixth as strong on the Moon as it is on EARTH. In ORBIT its weight would be zero, because the VELOCITY in orbit is enough to balance the pull of gravity.

force of gravity
on Earth

force of gravity
on Moon

in space

▲ On Earth, the pull of gravity gives an astronaut weight. Gravity on the Moon is weaker, so the same astronaut will weigh less. Floating free In space or in orbit, the astronaut is weightless.

wheel

The earliest method of moving huge blocks of stone was on wooden rollers. Later, people used solid wooden wheels instead. The wheel is one of the most important early inventions.

1–3

4–5

6–7

0

▲ Wind strength is measured by the Beaufort wind scale. Forces 1–3 are 'light breezes', just strong enough to rustle leaves.

wind

Winds are air CURRENTS produced by AIR moving between areas of different PRESSURE in WEATHER systems. In the northern hemisphere they swirl anticlockwise around a low-pressure area. But in the southern hemisphere of the EARTH the movement is the other way round. Windmills are a way of using wind power to generate ELECTRICITY. A wind tunnel is a chamber with a powerful fan, which is used to test the air resistance of model cars, AIRCRAFT and ROCKETS.

▶ Forces 10–11 are 'storm winds' that cause damage to buildings. The strongest wind in the Beaufort scale is force 12, a hurricane. Hurricanes travel at over 150 km/h.

◀ Winds blowing at up to 61 km/h are classified as 'strong winds'. They make large trees sway and to make walking difficult. A force 8 gale can blow slates off roofs.

◀ Force 4–5 winds are 'moderate winds', making trees sway and raising small waves on lakes.

word processor
A word processor is a COMPUTER which is used to create and print documents. The SOFTWARE allows you to correct what has been typed. Word processors have a keyboard similar to a typewriter, but with extra keys to edit, move and save text in the computer's memory. The words are shown on a screen, and in many systems there is a dictionary to check spelling automatically.

Wright Flyer
The Wright Flyer was the world's first successful powered plane. It was built by Wilbur and Orville Wright. The Wright brothers were bicycle builders who went on to design planes. They experimented with gliders and then on 17 December 1903 they made the first controlled FLIGHT in a heavier-than-air craft. It took place at Kitty Hawk in North Carolina, USA and lasted 12 seconds.

▼ The *Flyer 1*, built by Orville and Wilbur Wright, was the first successful powered aeroplane. Their achievements influenced aircraft designers in Europe and the United States for many years.

X

Y

x-rays

X-rays lie between ULTRAVIOLET and gamma RADIATION in the electromagnetic spectrum. They have a wavelength of less than a thousand millionth of a metre. This is smaller than an atom, and x-rays can pass through soft materials. X-rays cannot pass through bone, so they are used to photograph broken bones. They can show up the lining of the stomach and intestines with the aid of BARIUM meal.

xylol

Xylol (also known as xylene) is an example of a PETROCHEMICAL. Xylol can dissolve some PLASTICS and is also used in preparing specimens for the MICROSCOPE.

year

A year is the time it takes the EARTH to move in ORBIT once round the SUN. A year is exactly 365.25636 days long. To make up the extra quarter day, the month of February has 29 days (instead of 28) every four years. This is known as a leap year. As this makes the year slightly too long, there is no leap year in the first year of a century, unless it can be divided by 400.

▼ A year is the time taken by the Earth to orbit the Sun, about 365.25 days. Because the Earth is tilted on its axis, the two hemispheres lean towards the Sun and have summer at different times of year. Summer begins on 21 June in the northern hemisphere, and on 21 December in the southern hemisphere.

zero
Zero means nil. Early systems of NUMBERS had no zero. The Ancient Romans did not use it, for instance. Zero was thought up in the East about 1200 years ago.

zinc
Zinc is a soft, white METAL which does not react with the AIR. If sheets of STEEL are dipped into molten zinc, they are said to

▼ Zinc and zinc alloys are used to make dry battery cases, machine parts and some coins.

be galvanized. The steel does not rust for many years. Zinc is used to make old-fashioned carbon BATTERIES.

zircon
Zircon is a semi-precious stone. It is a form of ZIRCONIUM silicate and can be found in many different colours.

zirconium
Zirconium is a metallic ELEMENT with a very high melting point of 2130°C. It is used in nuclear reactors and the lining of JET ENGINES.

zone
A zone is a region with a recognizable character. The term is used in GEOGRAPHY to divide up the land.

zoom lens
A zoom lens is one which allows you to close in and magnify one part of a picture, without changing your position. The distance between a lens and the image it forms of a far off object is the focal length. In technical terms, a zoom is a LENS in which the focal length can be changed without altering the focus. See **photography**.

▼ A zoom lens can produce different pictures of the same scene. A 210mm setting magnifies part of the picture taken on a 75mm setting.

picture taken with 210mm zoom lens

picture taken with 75mm lens

Index

Page numbers in italics refer to illustrations.